Words for the Taking

Words

for the

Taking

—

THE HUNT FOR A PLAGIARIST

Neal Bowers

W. W. NORTON & COMPANY
New York London

Lines from "Tasting the Wild Grapes" excerpted from *American Primitive* by Mary Oliver. Copyright © 1978, 1979, 1980, 1981, 1982, 1983 by Mary Oliver. First appeared in *The Western Humanities Review.* By permission of Little, Brown and Company.

For information about permission to reproduce selections from this book, write to Permissions, W. W. Norton & Company, Inc., 500 Fifth Avenue, New York, NY 10110.

The text of this book is composed in 10.25/14 Palatino
Composition and manufacturing by The Maple-Vail Book Manufacturing Group
Book design by Susan Hood

Library of Congress Cataloging-in-Publication Data
Bowers, Neal, 1948–
Words for the taking : the hunt for a plagiarist / Neal Bowers.
p.   cm.
ISBN 0-393-04007-0
1. Bowers, Neal, 1948–   —Authorship.   2. Poetry—Publishing—United States—History—20th century.   3. Plagiarism—United States—History—20th century.   4. Poetry—Authorship—History—20th century.   5. Poets, American—20th century—Biography.   I. Title.
PS3552.08732Z462   1997
811'.54—dc20

[B]   96-15752
                                                   CIP

W. W. Norton & Company, Inc., 500 Fifth Avenue,
New York, NY 10110
http://web.wwnorton.com

W. W. Norton & Company, Inc., Ltd., 10 Coptic Street,
London WC1A 1PU

1 2 3 4 5 6 7 8 9 0

FOR NANCY,
WHO SHARES THIS STORY
AND A LIFE

Contents

Acknowledgments

I OWE SPECIAL thanks to Joseph Epstein, whose publication of my essay in *The American Scholar* gave me back my voice and led to the production of this book. Thanks also to Michael Bugeja for his wise counsel and unfailing friendship.

Editors George Core, Frederick Morgan, Joseph Parisi, and Peter Stitt have been and remain indispensable allies. Journalists William Grimes, Jan Harayda, Scott Heller, and Thomas O'Donnell did more than report my story; they took a genuine interest in it.

And Carol Houck Smith, whose sure hand guided me through the various drafts of this book, gave me the rarest of gifts—a clearer understanding of my own story.

Preface

IN A RECENT archaeological dig through old boxes stored in the attic crawl space, I discovered a page torn from the greater Galway phone book, a ragged sheet from the M's, and sat there pitched forward on my knees in the half-darkness trying to determine its importance. Midway down the queue of names, a little check by one of the Murphys worked its Rosetta Stone magic, and a moment in Ireland 15 years ago came rushing back. "Richard Murphy, Poet." I had ripped the page as proof that Irish poets can claim for themselves a special status in their homeland. Nothing in the malled and office-parked towns of America encourages our bards to single themselves out for such public distinction.

American poets have trouble admitting they are poets, partly out of humility but also because mere mention of the word poetry makes everyone remember a prior appointment. It's a sure conversation stopper at the Cyclone Lounge or in the neighbor's kitchen, leading in either place to an uncomfortable silence or the mechanical recitation of a verse tattooed onto memory in the eighth grade: "Half a league, half a league, half a league on-ward." For this reason, I am filled with apprehension about the announcement I must now make: I am a poet. Worse than that, I am a poet whose poems have been pla-giarized.

My relatives and neighbors have long since adjusted to the first of these assertions. I was always a strange boy, different, quiet, they say. Of course, had I turned out to be a professional card shark they would remember me as wild and full of risk. Looked at in reverse, anybody's life seems inevitable; and if things don't align in just the right way, well, that's ironic inevitability. The second assertion, about plagiarism, is taking some getting used to. That anybody would steal my poems is shocking to my aunts and uncles—not because they care for poetry so much but because they believe stealing anything to be wrong. They have an old-fashioned belief in fair play. Among my friends and associates who claim to value poetry, how-ever, there is less certainty about right and wrong, particu-larly in the academic community, where "values" are sometimes defined as "biases." One of my colleagues recently told me I am "too principled" for my own good, a remark I took as a mixture of complaint and warning and which left me feeling imprinted by my upbringing and strangely guilty.

By either group's standards, however, my situation is extraordinary. Between 1992 and 1994, a person calling himself David Sumner had two of my poems accepted as his own 20 times at 19 different literary magazines. After learning of his activities, I managed to stop 9 of the publi-cations, but my poems still appeared in print 11 different times under someone else's name. For two years, my wife and I pursued this mysterious thief, uncovering the theft of other poets' works along the way but finding no one else plagiarized more than once. It seemed I was his favorite poet, which was a privilege akin to having a tapeworm.

David Sumner proved to be one of several pseudonyms he used. He pretended, at various times, to be living in Japan, to be his own brother, and to be some other David Sumner. Whenever we got a grip on his shirttail, he turned into a pile of somebody else's laundry. Eventually he disappeared altogether. During the time we chased him, he never acknowledged responsibility for his actions; and he offered no rationale for stealing poems by Mark Strand, Sharon Olds, Marcia Hurlow, and Robert Gibb in addition to mine. It seems likely he is still engaged in his peculiar trade under another assumed name. The quarterlies are already littered with his primary pseudonym—57 known poems attributed to David Sumner in 46 periodicals, perhaps all of them other people's work.

Because I came of age in the 1950s and saw enough cowboy movie "flesh wounds" to know I'm supposed to be stoic and silent about my own injuries, I admit to feeling very unlike Randolph Scott as I set about telling this story. I also know that as much as I learned to admire those tough men with their bloodless bullet holes, I have been conditioned to dismiss the victim. Our culture has a great appetite for profiles and biographies of assorted felons, but victims rarely qualify for even secondary interest. Perpetrators of crimes are people of action, while those they injure are essentially passive, obscured from view by the dark attraction of their antagonists. We seldom ask how the victim feels or what he will do, although we speculate endlessly about why the villain "did it" and often get caught up in the mechanics of how it was done. The victim is necessary but does little more than introduce us to the person who has misused him.

Deprived of his voice as well as his work, the victim of plagiarism is almost always quiet. Why he doesn't tell his tale is a complicated matter, but it begins with the disparity between his own astonishment and outrage at having been robbed and the indifference with which many regard his plight. "Lighten up," they say, "no big deal." Responding to my excited cries, one of my colleagues actually told me, "Relax, you can always write another poem."

Let me state plainly, I do not wish to equate plagiarism with any capital offense. In fact, it probably doesn't hold its own alongside the lesser felonies, as I'm sure anyone who has had his life savings stolen by a con artist will attest. Going up a scale of seriousness in this way, though, is to invoke the it-could-be-worse consolation. Got a broken leg? It could be worse; you could have two broken legs. But the poor fellow hobbled by a cast and unable to scratch behind his knee knows his situation is bad enough. Poking futilely with his straightened coat hanger, he may feel like winding it around the neck of anyone who says anything about how much worse paralysis would be.

When a poem is stolen, the creative process itself is mocked, and the victim must defend not only his individual poem but also the very ground from which that poem arises. The most insidious aspect of plagiarism is how much damage it does to the surrounding terrain. Failing to understand the extent of the injury, those who hear the victim's complaints and regard them as extravagant worsen the loss. Focusing on the poem as property with little value, they become the plagiarist's accomplices after the fact, robbing the victim of his sense of worth. Faced with this further deprivation, the poet must first declare that his work has been stolen and then argue that it matters.

This is the position in which I find myself, obliged to offer not merely a defense of my creative work but also of poetry's worth. Mine is the tale of how a relentless plagiarist affected the life of one poet and how his activities reverberated across the literary and academic terrain, revealing fault lines. Among the characters populating the landscape are personal friends and relatives, an assortment of poets and editors (some famous and some unknown), various members of the legal profession (variously effective), a private investigator who appears guileless but is cagey enough to make P. D. James proud, and a sociopathic thief. They and others carry their individual parts of a narrative, including tape recordings of the plagiarist, clandestine moves across international borders, faked addresses and identities, a box of fabricated documents, inflated billable hours, and a six-month tour of prison. Woven through all is the thread of my wife Nancy's involvement. Never tiring on the journey as I sometimes did, she gathered information and kept the records without which most of the details contained in this book would have been lost.

Here, too, is an affirmation of what matters most to the poet, the process and the work it enables, those moments when the word and the world are one thing, an utterance against silence. Poetry is every bit as mysterious to me as it is to the person who knows little or nothing about it, but that is its essential attraction. Having never been satisfactorily defined, "poetry" is as ineffable as the meaning of life, something understood only in the experience and only then in ways that can never be fully communicated. To write poems is to be continually humbled and amazed by the process—a unique blend of intent and accident, the two things coinciding because of the poet's labor, as when a man digging a place for jonquil bulbs in his backyard unearths a meteorite.

Think of me with my soiled knees, one more unattested poet in the pages of the phone book, busy about my work because it matters to me. Whatever envy I feel for Richard Murphy and the regard his Irish townsfolk have for what he does is only a passing twinge. But the lack of community, even among my fellow writers and editors, has made it difficult to defend myself against the person who has stolen my poems. Many of those from whom I expected support took the part of the plagiarist, expressing concern for him as a misguided or tortured individual. Some accused me of laying false charges, some of being arrogant in the defense of my creative property, and some simply never responded to my call for help.

Of course, I had some true friends and supporters along the way, but the integrity of a system cannot be validated by the times it works as it should. If it periodically fails, the failures are far more significant and warrant investigation. So if I dwell upon the wrongs I experienced at the hands of my literary and academic fellow creatures, I do so not out of bitterness (though I confess feeling some residual resentment) but out of a sincere wish to make things better.

Presented here is an account of an extraordinary period in my life, a victim's story but also the story of an earnest maker of poems. The viewpoint is personal rather than historical, local rather than universal. Unlike most accounts of plagiarism, this one focuses on the effects of the plagiarist's acts upon a person he has wronged. It is a story thrust upon me by circumstance, and I relate it out of a stubborn rejection of silence, affirming my work in the small town where my life as a poet, though not officially noted in any public document, is nonetheless made possible.

Words for the Taking

1.

Out of Nowhere

FOR NEARLY twenty years, I have led a mostly uneventful life in Ames, Iowa, a town far from the reaches of big city noise, a place where many of my neighbors leave their front doors unlocked even at night. And though some of us who are not native to this place are more cautious, perhaps a little less trusting in the fates or the goodness of our fellow human beings, even we have been lulled by the herd effect of so much complacent security. And why not? Most of our local crime is of the drunk and disorderly variety, which is cited in the Arrest Report section of the newspaper each week, along with violations of the noise ordinance and an occasional simple battery. These excesses occur primarily among the 24,000 students who attend Iowa State University and seem more the product of youthful exuberance than of malice. Nothing to worry about, I tell myself late at night as the trains rumble through, sounding their deep-toned horns at the edge of town in salute to our dreams, and I sometimes wish for the simple trust it would take to get up and open all my doors as a token of community.

Being a poet compounds the uneventfulness of my life, simply because poets in our culture are mostly ignored. No volumes of poetry make the bestseller list, and Rod McKuen is the last poet I can recall seeing on a commercial television talk show, back in the days when he was packaging melancholy with his shot rocker's voice and selling it to the sensitive masses. Come to think of it, McKuen is probably the best example of why "celebrity poet" is an oxymoronic term. Most of us lead lives of quiet inspiration, blessed by the calling that damns us to obscurity. During the times when I am not teaching and have extricated myself from the latest ad hoc committee charged with reinventing the university, I can be found at home with a yellow legal pad in my lap, writing or trying to write poems. Usually, I'm wearing pajamas, as my neighbors who have grown used to seeing me retrieve the afternoon paper looking as if I had just got up will attest. Things are that sedate around here.

Poetry is a quiet passion, happening at odd moments in out of the way places. Apart from the occasional vision of something lovely and whole, like a meadow glimpsed between mountains, the process is a slow climb. Much of the time, it's downright tedious. Hard work, I would say, but for the example of my father, who labored all his life, and my mother, who still puts in 56 hours a week during peak season at the yearbook factory. By comparison, my flannel afternoons seem pure indolence, especially with a cat asleep on my outstretched legs.

Of course, no life is entirely idyllic, and mine is infrequently marred by the memo wars and meetings initiated by colleagues at the university. They talk with the earnestness of pallbearers about how to devise another committee to undertake a study that will result in the formation of another committee. And the poetry world, too, brings disruptions and frustrations, most of them tinged with the politics of petty in-fighting over too little turf for too many practitioners, none of the disputes of any consequence to anyone outside our tiny domain. But one grows accustomed to these irritations, as one accepts, grudgingly, the nasal whine and endless talk of a doddering aunt, because she is, in spite of whatever is wished to the contrary, a relative. In time, it is possible to tune her out while nodding politely as if paying attention, a technique I have nearly perfected but which has conditioned me to be a poor listener in general.

Nancy, my wife, refers to my moments of inattention as "being in that other world," the realm to which I presumably retreat when I'm thinking of poems. Most of the time, of course, like everyone else, I'm thinking of nothing in particular or maybe wondering what kind of music would have sprung from a Jim Morrison / Jacques Brel collaboration, which leads me to ponder the coincidence of their French connection, when Nancy penetrates my reverie with a question and I flounder once more on the beach of the rediscovered world. The best that can be said of me in these moments of re-entry is that my face is the face of Columbus as he splashed onto the sand, a mixture of wonder and bravado.

Because I know myself too well, it is impossible for me to think of the poet as someone especially gifted. I certainly don't feel blessed by the fates or beset by the furies, and I grow weary of the popular image of the poet as someone different. That person in line at the supermarket, the one with the wan and wistful look, is more likely to be a farmer than a poet (at least around here). Set him to talking and you'll find he's as full of metaphors as the next guy, and what he sometimes feels when he looks out over the land, the sun perhaps flattened on the horizon like a drop of mercury and the night beginning, is as inexpressible as the best poem. Usually, he doesn't say anything, though the sensation may ring him like a bell, and when the resonance stops he goes back to his work in silence.

The poet is unable to let such moments pass without comment. Confronted with the ineffable, his task is to discover the words that will almost say, in their failing, what can never be said. Such work requires a kind of stubbornness, maybe even foolishness, and there are times when the effort seems presumptuous to the poet himself. Most days, I don't feel like one of mankind's unacknowledged legislators. In my worst moments, I worry I am more like the kid shooting baskets alone while giving a running commentary on the "game" as if broadcasting: "And now Bowers pulls up short for the close jumper. Scores!" No one is listening, and the game is a fiction. Still, if I stood behind the farmer at the grocery checkout and said, "When the sun sets here the whole sky tilts west, pours itself over the edge, draining toward a single point, and goes completely dry," there is the chance it might stir in him a recognition. This is the hope of the poet.

Such immediate communication and potential connection are all but impossible, of course, and the poet's work goes out to the world in literary periodicals and small books with no assurance it ever reaches anyone. Response from readers other than family members and personal friends is so rare that word from a stranger is an occasion for joy. So when I picked up my voice-mail messages in late January 1992 and found among the verbal clutter the voice of Carrie Etter, a poet unknown to me then living in Santa Monica, my spirits rose despite the overall import of her message. She said she knew my poems well enough to recognize my voice and style and felt certain she was in possession of a published poem that belonged to me but had someone else's name on it. She offered to fax the poem to me and left her phone number.

My first reaction was to feel flattered. Here was a poet in California who knew my work well enough to think she would recognize it even if it bore someone else's name. Not bad, I thought, to write in such a distinctive way, to be so completely myself that someone approaching my style would appear to be a plagiarist. And that was my initial conclusion. Having no hard evidence in hand, I assumed Carrie had stumbled upon a poem written in my style but not stolen from me. It was a good feeling, and I sat in my office for a long time before dialing her number, happy with the winter sunlight slanting in over my window-ledge garden of cacti.

When I phoned, I didn't ask Carrie to read the poem but simply gave her the department fax number. Our conversation was pleasant and brief, and as I waited afterwards for her page to glide down the wires from sunny Santa Monica to frozen Ames, Iowa, the good feeling persisted. An actual poem of mine, or at the very least my poetic voice, had lodged in her head and made her think she had discovered a thief. Would I recognize myself in the poem she was sending, or would I shake my head and wander off in amazement, the way I did when some mutual friends once introduced me to the person they insisted was my double? Neither of us noted any special similarities and, after a few awkward moments, parted like the strangers we were. What if the poem racing through climate changes and nearing the machine at my elbow turned out to be a boring thing with not one good feature? Better it were mine and stolen than wretched and mistaken for mine.

What the machine slowly released, with its last little tug on the end of the page, was a greater shock than I was prepared to receive. Except for the title, the first line, and a few minor differences in the body of the text, I held in my hand a verbatim transcription of one of my poems. The name on it was David Sumner, and it had been published in the December 1991 *Mankato Poetry Review,* but it was my poem. Some of my colleagues were milling around the room, making copies and looking at their mail, and I turned to one of them and said, "I've been plagiarized." I must have had on my face a smile of disbelief, because the response was delivered with a smile and a tone of incredulity, "Really?" All I had to offer as evidence was the single page, with someone else's name on it, so I heard my voice insisting, "Yes, really." I realize now the recipient of my declaration initially must have thought I was setting up a joke and merely played his part as straightman. At the moment, though, I felt decidedly unfunny.

Back in my office, I quickly found the September 1990 *Poetry* in which my poem originally appeared. I read each poem and then laid them side by side and read them a line at a time for direct comparison. In more than 20 years of college teaching, I had never seen a more flagrant example of plagiarism, and I kept thinking I would discover the joke my colleague had anticipated, something that would allow me to laugh the whole thing off.

SOMEONE FORGOTTEN

He is too heavy and careless, my father,
always leaving me at rest-stops, coffee shops,
some wide spot in the road. I come out,
rubbing my hands on my pants or levitating
two foam cups of coffee, and I can't find him
anywhere, that beat-up Ford gone.
It's the trip itself that blinds him,
black highway like a funeral ribbon
leading to the mesmerizing end,
his hands like Vise Grips on the wheel
and following, until he misses me,
steers wide on the graveled shoulders,
and turns around.
This time he's been gone so long
I've settled in here—married, built a house,
started a family, stopped waiting to see him
pull into the driveway though the wind
sometimes makes a highway roar high up
in the branches,
and I stop whatever I'm doing and look up.

—*David Sumner*

———

TENTH-YEAR ELEGY

Careless man, my father,
always leaving me at rest-stops,
coffee shops, some wide spot in the road.
I come out, rubbing my hands on my pants
or levitating two foam cups of coffee,
and can't find him anywhere,
those banged-up fenders gone.

27

It's the trip itself that blinds him,
black highway like a chute
leading to the mesmerizing end,
his hands locked dead on the wheel
and following, until he misses me,
steers wide on the graveled shoulders,
turns around.
This time he's been gone so long
I've settled in here—married,
built a house, planted trees for shade,
stopped waiting to see him pull into the
    drive—
though the wind sometimes makes a high-
    way roar
high up in the branches, and I stop
whatever I am doing and look up.

                        —*Neal Bowers*

Everyone who teaches basic courses in writing has a standard admonition for plagiarism. When I taught freshman composition in the early 1980s, I referred to it as my thou-shalt-not-steal spiel. It was serious business, but I had presented the warning so many times I had begun to mock myself, the way a weary actor sometimes does in a bad role. One whole class period early in the term would be given over to a definition of plagiarism and a stern lecture on why it is the academic world's equivalent of a capital offense. Invariably at least one student would express concern that true originality is impossible, and I would jokingly refer him to the philosophy department while reminding him that any thief knows when he puts something into his pocket that doesn't belong to him. It seemed that simple.

Over the years, I persuaded myself that most instances of student plagiarism resulted from ignorance rather than willful theft. Here and there I found pilferings—nothing substantial, nothing deserving formal censure. Like everyone who teaches, I heard the apocryphal stories of major heists: the story lifted from *Seventeen* and not discovered as a plagiarism until after it won a contest and was published in the student literary magazine, the thesis cobbled from so many different texts it read like a schizophrenic monologue. Colleagues still swap these accounts like gothic tales or items from "Ripley's Believe It Or Not," and they are mentally shelved alongside the wild child from Yellowstone and the man who ate an entire tree. Curios from the bent dimension.

During all those wise-guy presentations on plagiarism to assorted undergraduates, I never imagined my work would be stolen. The novel and screenplay are vehicles with flashy hubcaps and plush interiors on their way to or from the bank, but the poem is a plain sedan pulled over on the shoulder for a moment of reflection or the scenic view. The poverty of the art itself was my guarantee of safety. Why would anyone steal a poem when the price it commands on the open market varies from a single free contributor's copy to several dollars a line? And if someone were going to steal poetry, why would he steal mine? Who was David Sumner, anyway? These were the questions that nettled, but the one causing immediate discomfort was What now?

Bound up with my indignation and the feeling that my private life had been invaded was a wish for it all to go away. I worried that after the climax of revelation would come a messy denouement, and I understood for the first time why the victim so often drops the charges. Also, in the interest of my emotional health, and my arteries, I had recently vowed to avoid the stress of confrontations with sarcastic waiters and pompous deans, to be slower to dive for the lure dragged over the scummy bottom. Even though what I felt was no momentary adrenaline rush to prop the buffeted ego but a deeper wound, I still wanted to calm myself into a benign dismissal of the whole situation.

The poem itself wouldn't let me do that. Written in the tenth year following my father's unexpected death, it was meant as an affectionate memory of him and an expression of my ongoing sense of loss. I tried to take emotional risks in writing it, to do more than offer a collection of pocket lint gathered in an idle hour. His sudden death had felt to me like an abandonment, and I realize now, looking back at the poem, that the opening words, "Careless man," reveal the sense of betrayal I hadn't consciously acknowledged even at the time I wrote the poem. If he had been more careful, if he had not continued to smoke even after the doctor's warnings, if he had cared more for us, his family, if . . .

The poem was a bittersweet bloom I planted on my father's grave. The thief dug it up, pruned it to his liking, and damaged the roots in the process. Worse, he replanted it in the soil mounded over my father and pretended the loss was his. This was a mockery I could not endure. Smirking at me were the incompetent title change, ambiguous in the wrong way, as it suggests the father is forgotten, a direct contradiction of the poem's content; the incongruent clause "He is too heavy" in the opening, bastardized line, which makes my father a burden; the simile, "black highway like a chute," deformed to "like a funeral ribbon," representing death as a winding Sunday cruise rather than a headlong rush with no exit; and the stupid comparison of his hands to "Vise Grips" in place of my own haunting sense of their being "locked dead on the wheel." As a final corruption, the thief substituted "started a family" for my "planted trees for shade," thereby destroying the implied passage of many years, which becomes apparent in my poem when the trees are referred to near the end as being tall enough for the wind to roar "high up in the branches."

Children know they may have to preside over the deaths of their parents, but the logical anticipation of loss cannot prepare them for their actual graveside stand, especially if death is sudden. My father died in his own backyard in the middle of the afternoon and was found by a next-door neighbor. "A massive heart attack," my brother said when he phoned me, and the line we held between us seemed to pass through immense darkness. We gripped either end, and I remember slumping against the wall where I stood and sliding to the floor. After that, things come back in fragments: the long drive to Tennessee, my mother's hopeless face, the red dirt of the grave.

Small towns have their self-appointed funeral attenders, elderly women, usually, who go to the final rites of friends and strangers alike. These rituals fill their days and give solace, perhaps. Some of them were probably there the day we buried my father, indistinguishable from great-aunts in their print dresses and small hats, their formal sadness mingled with my family's grief. They, too, are dead by now, embraced by ceremony and earth. I grant them their place in the cortege, in the cemetery amid so many they never knew, alongside my father. David Sumner was not one of them, but now I am obliged to imagine him there, too. He has crashed the procession. At the grave site he stands with his hands folded in front of him, pretending to feel.

To put a shoulder under one side of the coffin and help bear the weight of the dead is to feel in the knees and along the spine the full force of loss. Those relatives and family friends who hefted my father with his exploded heart and took him to the last place were bowed by the literal death of him and would feel it in their own bones when they lay down that night. No poem can say what they knew in their very marrow, the end beyond the red-dark terror. In my grief I saw them stumble toward the hole and knew only my grief, which was all I could utter after a decade.

Most poets try to put up a good front, wishing to appear composed and self-assured; and everyone knows it takes a certain confidence to write anything. Behind the façade, however, poets are always trying to shake the hounds of doubt. Writing a poem often feels like pitching a tent in the Parthenon. The little, temporary shelter looks pathetic, almost comic, in the context of such massive history. At the very least, the poet risks neglect; at the worst, ridicule. But no criticism is as devastating as the poet's own feeling that he should be chased off the premises. That's why too often he makes a spectacle of himself, singing drunkenly in the ruins, spray-painting his name on the columns like a common vandal.

The real risk for poets is in the presumption of their art, not in any overt decision to live life dangerously. This could probably be said of all creative people, but poets seem to suffer it with a singular pang. Our secret is we have no secrets. Our knowledge is an absence of knowledge. What we possess is faith in a process that leads us somewhere and often gives us the chance to take much more credit than we know we deserve. Mind emptied of intent, the poet surprises himself, knows himself to be fortunate to say the things he says, knows the poem is infinitely smarter than he is.

Simply thinking of telling people about my plagiarized poem triggered latent insecurities. Beyond the implied value of the poem itself, I would have to state plainly that someone had stolen something of worth. Otherwise why would the thief have bothered? Surely no one would steal a poem that wasn't good. I would also have to state emphatically that the poem was mine, immodestly representing myself as the wronged author.

Needing to show proof of plagiarism to someone and, perhaps, to gauge reaction, I took the faxed poem and the copy of *Poetry* containing "Tenth-Year Elegy" and went back to the mailroom in search of colleagues. I put the evidence into the hands of two people, both of whom started grinning as they compared texts. Their expressions suggested disbelief and each said, "You've been plagiarized, all right," before walking off. Neither asked how I felt or what I would do, nor did they express curiosity about how I discovered the theft or who the thief was. Though I didn't see anything portentous at the time, this was the first sign of how little sympathy and help I would receive.

As soon as I could escape the building, I headed home, eager to show Nancy what I had told her about in a brief phone call. She knew "Tenth-Year Elegy" well enough not to need it for reference, and as I stood just inside our front door, unloading mail and memos from my briefcase, she read the fax, her face turning stern with disbelief. "This is your poem! Someone has stolen your poem!" she said. "Who would do such a thing? Why?" Nancy takes a proprietary interest in my poetry because, as the first reader of everything I write, she is unfailingly honest and won't let me by with anything less than my best effort. Still I was surprised by the degree of her distress, though her reaction is the one I would have felt had I been free of the ego's insecurities.

During dinner we talked of nothing but the plagiarism. Afterwards, we went to my office looking for other Sumner publications. At the time, I edited *Poet & Critic*, a literary magazine then based at Iowa State, and received dozens of exchange issues from other magazines. Having long since overflowed the shelves, they stood in stacks around my office and buried my work table. The search took on special importance, because I worried that Sumner might have sent poems to *Poet & Critic* and could conceivably defend himself by claiming I stole his original poem in manuscript and published it as my own.

Feeling vulnerable, I sat down before one stack of periodicals as Nancy began sifting through another. The search might have gone on for hours, except that chance led me to an issue of *Half Tones to Jubilee*, from Pensacola, Florida, within the first fifteen minutes of our ramble, and I saw the name David Sumner in the table of contents. Turning to the poems, I actually shouted when I recognized a poem of Mark Strand's with Sumner's name attached. Odd to feel such happiness at the discovery of another plagiarism, but this bit of thievery made it impossible for Sumner to accuse me. Moreover I now had company and so felt less isolated. The Strand poem was an often anthologized one, "Keeping Things Whole." Sumner had changed the title and first line, as he had done with my poem. He called it "The Reasons for Me," but it was essentially a verbatim copying of Strand's original.

The relief was only momentary, though, as Nancy and I began to realize what our new discovery meant. If two poems had been stolen, there were bound to be more; and, because a former poet laureate had been robbed, no one appeared safe. We dove back into the periodicals, and Nancy turned up one more alleged Sumner poem in an issue of *Sou'wester,* though we couldn't identify it as a definite plagiarism. Beyond these finds, the name David Sumner did not appear again that night, but we sat up late pondering who he was and what he was up to. Because the Strand plagiarism was so flagrant, I wondered if Sumner was playing a cynical game, publishing a famous poem to show he could get away with it and thereby illustrate how poorly read or inattentive editors and other poets are. He was out to make fools of us all, I concluded. But my poem certainly wasn't well known, and Sumner's appropriation of it couldn't be satisfactorily explained by my theory.

When I mentioned my predicament to my graduate class the next day, a young woman spontaneously offered to find the thief and break his kneecaps. Her suggestion of violence was out of character, but it represented a gender difference I saw in reactions to the basic facts of the case. From the beginning, men were inclined to be philosophical, while women reacted more forcefully, seeming to recognize in the act of plagiarism itself something personal, nearer to home. Perhaps their own vulnerability in a society where women are less safe than men makes them more empathetic. Nancy told me, long before we had any information about David Sumner, that she intuited he was an ingratiating manipulator, but her specific word for him was "creepy."

In those first few days I felt the way I do with a bad

cold—miserable but almost privileged. The aches and drizzles elicit attention, often sympathy, even if it isn't sincere: "There, there, poor thing. You must feel awful." Apart from one or two scholars, I had never known anyone who had been plagiarized, and I had certainly never heard of a more obvious case than my own. No ambiguity, no room for doubt, a full-blown infection; and the more I sniffled the more I was told I should be suffering my way to health in my own home, not out in public spreading germs. As always, the novelty of illness dissolved to pure misery, and in my fever I thought mostly of my father.

2.

The Reluctant Posse

MY FATHER was given to fantasies of retribution. After dinner, which he ate in a sweat as if it were an extension of his day's labors, he pushed back and lit his cigarette. Exhaling across the table, he sometimes catalogued the wrongs he had recently suffered and promised to get even: "That little yellow-bellied coward, I'm going to give him a piece of my mind. Yes sir, I'll let him know he can't push Floyd Bowers around. Just you wait and see." He must have known, even as he threatened a toe-to-toe, nose-to-nose resolution of his latest grievance it would never happen. In all the years I heard him fume and vow on his own good name, he never confronted anyone. Still he enjoyed such sweet rectitude, the thought of having the last word.

Bequeathed my father's bluff and bluster, I was convinced something had to be done to rectify my own situation, though I wasn't sure what that something was. I spent languid afternoons at home, when I should have been writing poems, fantasizing how my thief would react if he opened his door and found me there, armed with accusations and evidence. Unable to deny anything, he would capitulate and plead for compassion. Or maybe he would try to escape, and I would tackle him in the hydrangeas, where he would confess everything to a jury of nodding blossoms.

My father would have approved, and others shared this fantasy, coming by it independently. One friend offered the example of Gregory Orr confronting a thief of his poems, telling him to stop or else. This was the kind of *mano a mano* scene I had replayed in my mind, and I felt fortified by the story until I contacted Orr and learned it was untrue. He had, indeed, been plagiarized in the middle 1970s and recalled having several friends offer to intercede on his behalf, but no face to face encounter ever occurred. Instead a threatening letter from Orr's publisher, Harper and Row, produced a written apology from the plagiarist and his activities stopped. As for my florid fantasies, Orr advised against personal intervention, saying I might be "bumped off by a two-bit psycho."

The possibility that plagiarists are mentally disturbed is a common view, although the severity of the disorder is unknown. Most regard their activity as mild and harmless, akin to kleptomania, something we cannot condone but should look upon with a kind of parental compassion. Others see it as a more dangerous psychosis involving invasion of personal space, housebreaking with fetishistic implications. In either case, many advise that the best course may be inaction. Dwelling on the injury only makes it worse, as when someone cuts you off in traffic and you hit the horn while spraying your windshield with fricatives. Let it pass, and half-an-hour later the incident isn't even a memory. Make an issue of it and your seared synapses will sputter the rest of the day. What is worse, the offending driver may take a shot at you.

The fear of violence surrounding plagiarism has no basis in fact, and yet it persists. Friends who half seriously suggest intimidation to bring the thief to his senses worry, at the same time, about the physical danger he may pose. Because he doesn't follow the rules, he presents himself as reckless, possibly dangerous; and even though his thieving is performed long distance and not through direct contact with his victim, he bears enough resemblance to the second-story man to cause concern. Of course, his remoteness may induce tough talk among the victim and his friends. I recall promising to perform a headlock combined with short jabs to the nose if I could only get my hands on the culprit. This was an interesting threat considering my last physical confrontation came in eighth grade with a punk named Snake Frazier, who broke in front of me in the cafeteria line and said, "You don't mind, do you?" I lied and said I didn't, but I pummeled Snake mercilessly in my imagination.

Although separated by more than three decades, the junior high tough who took my space and the person signing his name to my poetry stand together because they belong to the same gang, the one whose motto is "Mine for the taking." Not for them the embezzler's clandestine erasures but the bold shouldering aside to stand in someone else's place. The last I heard, Snake was in the state penitentiary for pushing too hard (drugs and people). I secretly count a few months of his time as penance owed to me, months I'm sure the judge would have added had I appeared as an anticharacter witness for the prosecution. But no one called when Snake was having the latest of his many days in court.

Despite profound feelings of injury and my wish to

somehow set things right, everything outside my day-dreams argued for letting go. Counterpointing the possibility my thief might be dangerous was the equally dissuasive prospect that he might be pathetic, a down-and-out poet manqué with a bad shave and a quart of soured milk in his refrigerator. Driven not by malice but by something crooked under his disheveled hair, he was hard to view as an adversary. Surely he deserved as much compassion as the spiders and box elder bugs I capture inside the house and release on the lawn.

Working with all the clarity of a bad psychic, I concluded my villain was either a psychotic or a misguided kid with someone else's song in his heart. He was Charles Manson with a complete collection of Barry Manilow records. No sketch artist could render him as anything other than a caricature, and I realized I needed much more information about him before deciding what action to take. Not that any course of action is clearly defined for the plagiarized poet. After all, to whom should instances of plagiarism be reported? By what means can the aggrieved poet seek justice? Little wonder my options seemed limited to personal intervention or benign dismissal and that I couldn't make up my mind.

Looking for at least some measure of moral support, I contacted my fellow victim Mark Strand. Suffering no consternation at all, he replied, "I heard from some mag. in Florida about David Sumner and his plagiarism. They were worried about lawsuits, etc. I told them not to worry, that I really didn't care what Sumner did. It is, however, too bad—and very sad. I don't think he can build much of a career with plagiarized poems. He'll just keep being found out. Anyway, thanks for your letter." Told that Strand's editor at Knopf, Harry Ford, also considered the matter trivial, I began to feel petty and mean, as if I were bent on tracking down someone who stole a crust of bread.

Because our legal system makes distinctions between small-time larceny and grand theft, perhaps we should distinguish between trivial and significant instances of plagiarism. The determining factors might be the scope and nature of the stolen work, the stature of the periodical publishing it, and the amount of money the thief receives for representing it as his own. Or maybe some works could be identified as inherently all right to steal because their intrinsic value has been exhausted or because they were never very good in the first place. Whether Strand and Ford applied such measurements when they shrugged off David Sumner's plagiarism of "Keeping Things Whole," I don't know. I suspect they quite honestly didn't care that the poem had been stolen. The act was simply beneath their level of notice.

I wished for their aristocratic detachment, but it was already too late. I had committed my faux pas as irredeemably as the diner who screams fire when the flambe flares at the next table. "How déclassé," murmur the others, touching their napkins to their lips, "how drôle." The poor fool's only options are to retreat or laugh at himself and make the most of a miserable predicament. I chose the latter course, telling the story of my plagiarized poem locally so often it began to feel less like an experience than an invention, the way unusual events turn into embellished narratives over brie and cocktails. Nancy and I became such experts at presenting the tale we spontaneously yielded certain parts of it to one another in a seamless duet and could anticipate every question that would follow.

It was my father's strategy, his frustration and worry disguised as narrative. I recall him coming home from work one evening, worn out and obviously a little scared. Someone had opened the passenger door when he was stopped at an intersection and tried to get into the car with him. At first, he said he sped away, straight through the red light, but later he added the details of turning and putting his legs across the seat to keep the man out and then of actually kicking him back onto the sidewalk. The more he talked, the more he seemed to remember, including some movie-like dialogue between him and the voluntary passenger. By the time the dinner dishes had been cleared away, he was in complete control of the moment, never in harm's way.

I, too, wanted to boot my interloper but in reality just kept speeding off. During the three weeks immediately following Carrie Etter's call, the theft of a single poem grew small in the rearview mirror. The more I looked back at it the more it blended in with the overall landscape. Like my father's would-be rider, mine was anonymous, which made it easier still to flesh him out and clothe him in whatever fashion pleased me.

Friends and colleagues listened to my yarn, compared my poem with its plagiarized clone, and said, "Imitation is the sincerest form of flattery"; "You should feel complimented to have someone like your work well enough to steal it"; and "You know your poem is good because it has been published twice now." These and similar comments all fit the making-lemonade-when-life-hands-you-a-lemon perspective offered by various advice columnists. More than a platitudinous playback, though, there was in my consolers' tone something authentic, the suggestion that plagiarism really is a pat on the back and a boost to the ego; and they were often upset when I bristled or responded sarcastically.

Looking for professional commiseration, I wrote poet friends and acquaintances. Some, like Paul Zimmer, director of the University of Iowa Press, urged me not to get drawn so far into pursuing David Sumner that I would use up valuable writing time. Others, like George Core, editor of the *Sewanee Review,* advised me not to contact Sumner directly but to "have a little fun with him by sending him a semiliterate warning in which you have written out the message by using letters and words cut out from newspapers. Of course you wouldn't mention your poem but would instead mention Strand's. This will frighten him and he may give up this deplorable habit. (Be sure that the warning is posted from a town long from where you live.)" Steve Corey, associate editor of *The Georgia Review* and an old graduate schoolmate from the University of Florida, wrote, "Our two known cases of plagiarism both turned out to involve mentally disturbed people, and if that is the case, you'll no doubt end up dropping everything out of compassion. But if the guy is indeed launched on a malicious (and apparently extended) campaign, then I hope you can nail him."

Among the most interesting responses were those offering stories of plagiarism resulting from "honest" imitation and photographic memory. One such account in which the plagiarist used both rationales to defend himself involved Henry Taylor, whose poems were appropriated by a graduate student for part of his doctoral thesis. When Taylor protested the theft and argued that some form of censure was in order, he found the student's thesis committee more eager to avoid a messy academic situation than to hold the student accountable. Such evasion is typical of those in a position to punish plagiarists. Defending or exonerating on the thinnest rationales, they want to err on the side of fairness or, in many cases, simply wish to avoid unpleasantness. Plagiarism, after all, is ugly business, hard on the spirit, especially so for the victim, who wants justice and, at the same time, would like to be given some reason to relent.

My various, friendly counselors clearly had my welfare in mind when they wrote, but none had any practical advice for exposing the thief and setting the record straight. George Core was the only one with an actual plan, specific and outrageous, exactly the kind of cathartic fiction my father might have concocted, and it felt good to laugh a bit while picking at my Gordian knot. The absence of real guidance was, of course, a clear indication that there was nowhere to go.

Emergent in some of these friendly letters, however, was a surprising defense of the plagiarist and an admonishment for me to proceed with caution lest I hurt him unduly. If he were mentally disturbed, of course I would be cruel to punish him. But what plagiarist is entirely mentally healthy? Even more vexing, what if he were mentally gifted (or cursed) with the power to photograph text and couldn't distinguish between his own thoughts and words and those he had processed in the dark room of his mind? Perhaps photographic memory does exist in rare individuals, but it seems amazingly common as a defense against charges of plagiarism; and I have always wondered why the brain's Nikon never gets the name of the real author within its frame. Like the bad family photographer who lops the heads off his subjects, the plagiarist shoots low, preserving only the body. Later, flipping through his mental album, he points to every image, exclaiming, "That's me!"

With a multitude of disincentives bearing down on me, the heaviest was the thought of myself as an ungenerous egotist. Some sad, misinformed, deluded, gifted, disturbed, potentially violent, or naive and totally harmless person had paid me the compliment of liking my work enough to claim it, and I lacked the capacity of heart to understand and forgive. The more I thought of it, in fact, the more my distress seemed akin to jealousy, an emotion I rarely feel.

Like it or not, the ego drives the creative process, and creativity itself is a vain stay against mortality. Good or bad, every artist invests in the futures market, hoping his stock will yield dividends beyond his years. Even so, few writers sit down at their word processors or with their writing tablets and begin with the thought that they are making themselves immortal. And the vagaries of taste are as likely to elevate an obscure poet as they are to cast into disrepute a bestseller. So what's the big deal? Why should I be so possessive? The *Mankato Poetry Review,* which published the plagiarized version of "Tenth-Year Elegy," has a circulation of approximately 200. Not exactly *The New Yorker* lying on over 500,000 coffee tables. No portal to immortality here. So few people would ever see the stolen poem that, beyond the principle of the matter and the grumblings of my own ego, it nearly didn't count as a theft at all.

Because I hadn't told many people beyond Ames, I could still keep the story local, even though Nancy urged me to broadcast the news. She kept saying I needed to inform other editors of Sumner's activities so they could be on guard against him, and she encouraged me to write letters to trade publications such as *Poets and Writers* and the Associated Writing Program's *Chronicle*. Such notice would be a shrill whistle in a public place. Instead I put my hands in my pockets and sauntered deeper into the consoling shade of my big heart, which had room to shelter the plagiarist, too.

In less than a month I underwent a transformation akin to a religious conversion. The angry weather of vengeance had blown over and left me on the calm shore of forgiveness. Now, when I thought of David Sumner answering my knock at his door, I imagined him humbled by my benevolence. I might have grown entirely comfortable in this posture had a package not arrived from my friend Michael Bugeja, who suffered none of my uncertainty about what to do. Michael had searched for David Sumner's name among the magazines he received as editor of *Poet's Market*. Included in the short stack of pages he sent was another plagiarism of "Tenth-Year Elegy," published this time in *Poem*, again under the title "Someone Forgotten." All my goodwill hissed away. Seeing my poem represented a second time as David Sumner's convinced me this was not the work of an innocent. Even if he believed the poem to be his own, which seemed impossible, he had to know that the same poem should not be published in more than one periodical. Of course, since his plagiarisms were de facto multiple publications, his approach reflected a certain perverse logic.

Whatever Sumner's mental condition, deviousness seemed its central aspect. The evidence was there from the beginning, in the altered titles of my and Strand's poems, in the changed first lines, modifications which prevented easy recognition in a table of contents or index. This was no guileless cortical cameraman but a malicious thief, and I felt exquisitely gullible for conning myself into doing nothing. Now I was ready to sound the alarm.

In addition to *Mankato Poetry Review, Half Tones to Jubilee,* and *Poem,* which published Sumner plagiarisms, it was likely the other periodicals mentioned in Sumner's contributor's notes had been similarly abused. His biographical sketch in *West Branch,* one of the periodicals Michael Bugeja sent, provided some useful information:

> David Sumner, a.k.a. David Jones, lives in Aloha, Oregon. He was born in Belfast, Northern Ireland, and spent his childhood in England. His work has been published in *Hawaii Review, Puerto del Sol, Mississippi Review,* and many other magazines.

His note in *Poem* gave additional details, citing upcoming publications in *San Jose Studies* and *Seneca Review;* and Sumner claimed to have studied with John Gardner at Southern Illinois University and to hold a master's degree from Pacific University.

If these statements were true, he was no novice bumbling around in the world of poetry, but a shrewd and aggressive marketer of poems, successfully targeting the little magazines. My earlier notion that he was a cynical hustler out to make fools of as many editors and poets as he could was now more plausible than ever. I wrote immediately to periodicals mentioned in his contributor's notes and to others as well.

Mailing dozens of letters within a few days, I enclosed copies of my original poem and Sumner's retitled version to support my allegations. I sent along the Strand plagiarism as well, to show I wasn't suffering persecution delusions. My credibility was paramount when contacting editors who published poems by Sumner that could not definitely be identified as someone else's. The burden of proof was rightly mine, but establishing that Sumner had plagiarized two poems was not necessarily the same as earning an editor's trust.

Some of my letters were never answered, whether through incompetence or evasion I cannot say. Quite possibly some editors considered me a troublemaker and threw away my correspondence. Several responded that they had no intention of returning the Sumner poems they had on hand unless they were proved to be plagiarisms, which was comparable to accepting a chronic forger's check and assuming it to be good until it bounces.

Week by week, distressing news arrived, often disclosing still another plagiarism of my work. Deborah Tall, editor of *Seneca Review,* wrote that my letter came as she was going to press with yet another copy of my "Tenth-Year Elegy," this time titled "My Careless Father." She enclosed a second Sumner poem she had planned to publish, hoping I could identify it, too, as someone else's. Unbelievably, I found, it was another of mine, a poem originally titled "RSVP" and published in the same issue of *Poetry* as "Tenth-Year Elegy." Had my timing been a little slower, both poems would have appeared under Sumner's name, an almost exact replica of my original publication of them.

Sumner's appropriation of "RSVP" followed the same pattern as his theft of "Tenth-Year Elegy." Apart from the change of title and first line, the poem was lifted almost intact.

ASPECTS OF DEATH

The sky is shrouded, and death observes all
the courtesies, phones long-distance to say
he's dropped in on relatives, darkly hinting
he would like to visit me. Playing dumb,
I send flowers and make a small donation
to cancer research.

Not easily put off, he mediates a peace
between my brother and me. We haven't spoken
in three years but now swap snapshots
of our buried fears. No one could miss
the family likeness.

Moved by death, someone offers to cut
my grass, and most of my neighbors
bring food—so much pastry and potato salad
I can't eat it all before it spoils.

Finally, death persuades all my old lovers
to write "Sorry to hear of your loss" on cards
lightly scented where their perfumed wrists
rest while composing thoughts of sorrow.
Released by death, this sympathy floats
out of darkness, a beautiful moth beating
the black air back—I hear it now, powdering
the window as the telephone rings,
bringing maybe a local call, death in town
or down the block, but I can't answer
for the life of me.

                                        —*David Sumner*

———

RSVP

Death observes all the courtesies,
phones long distance to say
he's dropped in on relatives,
darkly hinting he would like
to visit me.
Playing dumb, I send flowers,
make a small donation
to longevity research.

Not easily put off, he mediates
a peace between my brother and me.
We haven't spoken in three years
but now swap snapshots
of our inmost fears.
No one could miss the family likeness.
Moved by death, someone
offers to cut my grass,
and most of my neighbors bring food—
so much pastry and potato salad
I can't eat it all before it stales or sours.

Finally, death persuades
all my old lovers to write
"Sorry to hear of your loss"
on cards lightly scented where
their perfumed wrists rest,
composing sorrow.

Released by death, this sympathy
floats out of darkness,
a beautiful moth beating the black air back—
I hear it now, powdering the window

as the telephone rings and rings,
bringing maybe a local call,
death in town or down the block,
but I can't answer for the life of me.

—*Neal Bowers*

Not substantial enough to disguise the poem, the altered line breaks and small editorial changes are perhaps meant as improvements: "cancer research" for "longevity research," "buried fears" for "inmost fears," and "spoils" for "stales or sours." One poet, comparing Sumner's plagiarism with my original, told me Sumner improved the poem's ending, as if being plagiarized were a workshop. That he saw something commendable in this destructive process was almost funny, a tired vaudeville routine in which the gag man says to his friend whose car has just been crunched, "Now it'll be easier to park."

As in "Tenth-Year Elegy," in "RSVP" I ponder my father's death. The poem is largely autobiographical. Although I felt relieved to have stopped its publication at *Seneca Review* and would have similar luck at *San Jose Studies*, I had too many falling plates to catch. The plagiarism would appear in six periodicals, most often under the title "Aspects of Death" but also as "Courtesies" and "The Visitor." "Tenth-Year Elegy" suffered a similar fate, intercepted before publication at five periodicals but published at five others under the titles "My Careless Father" and "Someone Forgotten." Other titles used for the intercepted plagiarisms were "My Father," "Father's Forgetfulness," and "Forgetfulness." Sumner so saturated the market with my two poems that I began finding his plagiarisms in periodicals to which I subscribed and in which I occasionally published. Shocking enough to discover myself plagiarized when consciously looking for stolen work, I was stupefied to turn the page while reading for enjoyment and see my own face, slightly distorted, looking back. The sensation was comparable to an experience I had years ago when rising in the night to investigate a strange noise. Half asleep, I turned full into my own reflection in a moonlit mirror. The face was mine but changed, eyes strangely dilated, face empty of personality, and the momentary horror of seeing myself as another produced an adrenaline jolt that kept me fanning the covers until daylight.

I continued writing editors, with mixed results. Roberta George, editor of *Snake Nation Review,* said she accepted a plagiarism of "Tenth-Year Elegy" and withdrew it after learning of Sumner's activities. She went on to observe, however, that "Our feeling was that this might be a young immature person or someone who had mental problems. In other words, everyone is guilty of something. Larry Brown has a wonderful story about being made to sleep with fat women for the crime of plagiarism." The attempt to explain away the plagiarist's activities as the manifestation of a mental disorder is familiar, but what have fat women done to deserve the ignominious curse of sleeping with plagiarists?

Things were taken even less seriously at *Whiskey Island Magazine,* which accepted and published Sumner's plagiarism of "Tenth-Year Elegy" after receiving a warning from me and copies of my original poem and its dented double. Having a copy of the plagiarism in hand in March 1992, the student editors accepted the identical poem only ten days later. When I discovered it in print and protested to the magazine's faculty advisor at Cleveland State University, I received no response. Follow-up letters likewise met with silence, although I did hear indirectly through a *Cleveland Plain Dealer* reporter, who later did a story on the case, that the student editor felt awful. She said she might have taken the warning more seriously except that it was the source of amusement among some of her professors and colleagues.

Harder to tolerate was a similar failure by one of my oldest and closest friends. Malcolm Glass, who coedits *Zone 3* and who for many years served as an editorial board member of *Cumberland Poetry Review,* received a warning from me with copies of all relevant materials and still published a Sumner poem in *Zone 3.* Worse, however, Glass voted to publish Sumner's plagiarism of "RSVP" in *Cumberland Poetry Review.* My protest letter about this put a strain on our friendship, because I was not in a mood to be patient and understanding. Malcolm's response, in his typical casual style, was essentially, "These things happen," and he later told me he initially thought the whole thing was funny.

Editors quite naturally assume that contributors are the actual authors of work they submit. In some cases, copyright forms declaring authorship are signed before publication, and Sumner often signed such statements before my poems went to press under his name. What is difficult to understand, however, is how editors can be victimized after being warned and given copies of the very poems they subsequently accept. Even the best intentioned seem inclined to regard accusations of plagiarism with skepticism, as perhaps they should. A wild claim is not the same as a substantiated case, however, and no one paying attention could possibly fail to see the difference.

Charges of plagiarism are never welcome, even among those who consider it a deplorable act deserving severe punishment. Most suspect the accuser of misinterpreting his situation or lying outright. Everywhere I was met with reservation and caution, often with dismissal. I couldn't have been made to feel less welcome had I been an official from the health department come to tell people they had been in contact with someone carrying a contagious disease. Like the whistle-blower who reveals corruption within an organization because he believes it is in everyone's best interest for the truth to come out, the person lodging charges of plagiarism becomes a pariah. Many of those most affected by his revelations, editors and publishers of periodicals duped by the thief, express gratitude, if at all, with their teeth clenched. And his colleagues become wary of him, wondering if he has become fanatical. More than a few friends advised me not to alienate editors by pushing my case too hard. Others cautioned me not to link my name too closely with plagiarism, even as a champion of right, because in the long-term people might not remember which side of the theft I was on.

These and other warnings made me modify my original fantasy of confronting Sumner. No doubt his neighbors would subdue me before I could tackle him, and I imagined myself sprinting across lawns and breaking through hedges to get away. I would be the stranger there, the troublemaker, and he the quiet writer seen by everyone working late into the night in an aura of light at his window. All the dogs would be barking and the kids running around wildly with sticks and flashlights as I huddled beneath the hydrangeas and panted to myself, "I'll get that yellow-bellied coward; just you wait and see."

3.

The Right Wrong Man

ALOHA. David Sumner lived in Aloha, Oregon. The town itself sounded whimsical, and I didn't fully believe in its existence until I checked an atlas and found its little dot among the stippled suburbs on the western edge of Portland. "Aloha," that serviceable Hawaiian word, means "love" and is used in greeting and departure, functioning as well for hello as it does for good-bye. On the map it looked like a practical joke, a wave across the distance from a figure I couldn't quite make out. Pure coincidence, I know, but it seemed a deliberate taunt; and as I pursued David Sumner I grew to appreciate the ironic doubleness of the word. Just as he seemed to be coming into view, he grew smaller on the horizon. Aloha.

Finding Sumner's address was as easy as checking my *Poet & Critic* logbook. Three different entries during the winter months of 1991 indicated that he submitted poems, all rejected by me or my assistant editor with whom I divided the chores of preliminary screening. Because Sumner was most actively circulating his plagiarisms during this time, it is likely the work we reviewed was stolen.

Worse is the possibility that he sent my own poems to *Poet & Critic* and they were read and rejected by my assistant editor. At the very least Sumner sent work to me at exactly the same time he was circulating my stolen poems to other periodicals. The perversity of this double injury seems grounded in a game of manipulation, as when the trusting dupe waits in the hotel lobby while the "guide" who has promised to show him the city loots his room. There I was, the fellow in the floral-print shirt, waiting by a dusty philodendron, studying the materials Sumner gave me while he descended the rear stairs and left the building with my valuables.

Knowing his whereabouts was a good start, and his considerable distance from Iowa relieved me of any lingering thoughts of paying him a personal visit. A letter would be the practical approach, but I soon learned that several of his victimized editors had written demanding an explanation of his actions and received no reply. Like me, they hoped for some rationale—not that he could reasonably establish his innocence, but that he would explain what he had been up to. The great unknown factor was his motivation, and I had a morbid fascination even for the lies he might tell. In my younger years as a teacher, I used to tell my students that although late papers were unacceptable I would be delighted to hear excuses for any assignments not handed in on time, provided the stories were original and colorful. In my more expansive moments, I even promised a higher grade for a really good tale. Crediting Sumner was unlikely, but I held out hope he might display greater invention than my tardy students, who never once won me over.

While I was considering my letter to Sumner, its proper tone and what concessions it should demand, word arrived from the editors of *Half Tones to Jubilee,* where the Strand plagiarism appeared, that Sumner was no longer in the United States. Allan Peterson, the magazine's editor, wrote: "We have written to Sumner and received no reply to our charges. He did, however, just submit a new batch of poems to us from Japan. Imagine. (The address is D. Sumner, Odawara, Kanagara, Japan.)" So much for my letter. If he was out of the country, he was beyond my reach. I could still write to him, of course, but the Pacific Ocean was a daunting divide.

Peterson and his associates had used razor blades to amputate the stolen Strand poem from all copies still on hand, so they were in no mood to allow Sumner in their magazine again. The only logical explanation for Sumner's new submission was that Peterson's letter exposing him as a plagiarist had not caught up with him in Japan before he offered other poems for consideration. A plagiarist as active as Sumner might well leave the country, the way embezzlers and stock manipulators go offshore to spend other people's money and avoid prosecution, but not everyone was gullible enough to accept the Japanese address at face value.

Jeanne K. Tsutsui, the editor-in-chief of *Hawaii Review* in 1992, responding to my general letter of warning to all periodicals cited in Sumner's contributor's notes as publication credits, told me of her attempt to return poems to Sumner using his own stamped, self-addressed envelope:

Someone perhaps Sumner (because it doesn't look like an official postal service label), had stuck on a label with a forwarding address to "Shiroyama, Odawara / Kanagara, Japan 250." The envelope had also been stamped "Returned for Postage / Air 56 Additional / Surface 41 Additional," but this was crossed out with a black marker, probably by the post office or our campus mailing service. The envelope had obviously reached Japan but was returned because of the insufficient address information of the label. It seems as if Sumner has gone into hiding—or is attempting to hide.

Her suspicion that Sumner himself stuck a bogus forwarding label on his own returned poems, knowing they would make their way back to her and implicitly establish his Japanese residence (albeit one to which mail was undeliverable), while he remained in Oregon, stirred my own doubts. It would be much cheaper and logistically simpler to fake a move than to make one.

Because plagiarism is itself a deception, I don't know why I was surprised Sumner might deceive people in other ways, except I had initially envisioned him as someone of limited imagination. Not that deviousness requires a large brain. The killdeer flies from her fledglings and fakes a crash, pretending to be wounded, to lead the curious hiker away. No great amount of cleverness was required for Sumner to cry out, "Japan! Japan!" flapping everyone off in the wrong direction. But he had been so inept as a plagiarist, not even leaving room for what the federal bureaucrats call "plausible deniability," that he seemed incapable of true guile. The "better" plagiarists know how to alter the language enough to create doubt about the theft. They steal ideas and practice paraphrase. Sumner's approach was less subtle, but it was hard to believe he was making up his moves as he went along. Surely he had a plan, one that allowed him to justify his actions to himself: "Those biased editors made me do it"—that sort of thing. Perhaps he was smarter than I imagined—smart enough to give the appearance of being dumb.

Speculation is its own labyrinth. Easy to take one turn too many and snap the slight thread of truth tied to the real world. I knew nothing of Sumner other than the brief information he provided in his contributor's notes, so fathoming his motives and coming to grips with his plans was a pointless enterprise. He might be as uncomplicated as the killdeer or as shrewd as a confidence man. The only way to know was to contact him, if not by mail, then by telephone.

Nancy volunteered to search for his number in the Portland phone book at the local library. She found, in the city itself and in several suburbs, a surprising number of Sumners. One even lived in Aloha, although his first name wasn't David and no street address was listed to compare with the one we had. She also made note of the David Joneses, since Sumner had given that name as one under which he sometimes writes. Of these, there was a David Jones, Sr., and a Jr.

Perhaps one of the numbers on her list would ring a phone in the plagiarist's home, but what would we say when he answered; and how would we make him reveal himself? We decided Nancy would place the calls, partly because she finds the telephone more agreeable than I do, but mostly because a woman's voice might take Sumner off guard. We considered having her pretend to be an editor or simply a poetry fan who had seen Sumner poems in the periodicals and wanted to talk with him. But in the end we opted for a more direct approach.

One by one, Nancy rang the numbers and asked for David Sumner and/or David Jones. She sounded like a telemarketer, and was regarded that way by some who picked up the receiver in and around the city of Portland. "What are **you** selling?" bled through their strained politeness, with the J. and D. Sumners turning out to be women, though they volunteered no information except a curt, "No David here," before hanging up. David Jones, Sr., was more talkative and laughed heartily when Nancy asked if he or his son, David, Jr., wrote poetry. Inquiring if they had ever bungee-jumped from Hoover Dam couldn't have produced a howl of greater incredulity.

The only yes to the poetry question came from a young man who said we had reached his sister's number and that her live-in boyfriend wrote poetry. Unfortunately his name was neither Sumner nor Jones, and we gathered he was known to scribble an occasional couplet on birthday and anniversary cards: "Another year has come and passed. / Whoever said it wouldn't last?" I prefer to think he specialized in the limerick rather than such verbal handcuffs, but many a local reputation has been made on less virtuosity.

The calls led us nowhere, and by the time Nancy hung up for good we realized she had been conducting a random survey. We could have accomplished the same thing by calling another name in another city—Richard Brown, for instance, in Detroit. Following that procedure enough times might yield data for a quirky sociological study revealing the likelihood of finding a poet at random, but it wouldn't uncover our plagiarist. The one David Sumner/Jones we were seeking was probably listed under another name or didn't have a phone. Maybe we would do better to call directory assistance in Japan.

In the end, Sumner's evasiveness led me to the law, almost in spite of myself. Because I couldn't find him and he seemed disinclined to respond to any charges laid against him through the mail, I felt I had no choice but to seek expert help, someone with special resources, someone who could apply the right kind of pressure and get results. I needed a lawyer. "Like a drowning man needs an anchor," said the cynical voice between my ears. But I grew desperate with the weekly discoveries of more plagiarisms. Sumner didn't intend to stop, and I needed help in the worst way, which, as the old joke goes, was just what I got.

Obtaining legal assistance was not as easy as thumbing through the Yellow Pages. Despite its vaunted reputation as a place filled with writers, Iowa contains few people knowledgeable about copyright law, as I learned in trying to enlist an attorney. Phone calls to a legal referral center netted several possibilities, but no one wanted to take the case or was even sure there was a case, per se. Ipso facto, good-bye. Our best hope seemed to be Bruce McKee, a Des Moines patent attorney, but his first question to us was, "Why don't you just phone up this Sumner and tell him to stop?"

Looked at dispassionately, McKee's opening query might have been a good sign. At least he wasn't eager to litigate if things could be settled simply. The possibility that he just didn't appreciate my predicament became more likely with his successive inquiries about the worth of a poem and why anyone would steal poetry if its value was purely intrinsic. What puzzled him most, however, was my sense of loss. How could I be so upset over an action which deprived me of nothing? I had not lost money. My home had not been broken into. Ergo, what did I expect him to do? Clearly, we had struck some rudimentary bottom, both logically and legally. Originally valued by *Poetry* at $2.00 per line, my work could not be made to appear financially valuable; and it was difficult to explain to a highly paid attorney that a professional poet could command no more than that for his work.

Instead of saying, "Me victim; you lawyer. Sue!" I tried to explain myself to McKee in writing. During the initial phone conversation, he had expressed almost no interest; but after receiving my apologia, he phoned to say he would try to help out. What brought him around, I suspect, was neither my fervent plea for assistance nor my argument for the integrity of my work but the presentation of myself as a writer and professor of at least some small distinction. Looking back, I understand why I felt I had to establish my credentials, to be taken seriously by someone who regarded my complaint as trivial. I oversold myself, giving the impression I was not simply someone to reckon with but also a man of means. I went so far as to make the following assertion: "I realize that it may end up costing me money, but the principles involved here are central to my life as a poet and a professional person. If I, as the person most abused by David Sumner, do not take steps to stop him, who will?" Intended to persuade McKee of my seriousness and sense of injury, I see now the statement can also be construed to mean "money is no object." And I was so excited to have real legal help I didn't think to ask about his rates. Ours was a match made in utter ignorance.

On the phone McKee resembled Jimmy Stewart more than Raymond Burr, his pinched, nasal voice making him sound like a man who could drill the truth out of anyone. Disarming but keen, I concluded, a devastating combination for the poor defendant. Sumner wouldn't have a chance against my Midwestern barrister, folksy and shrewd, with a wit as dry as the corn in autumn. I felt better just thinking of him, especially when I set about drafting, at his request, a complete description of the case. Nagging reservations about his ability to grasp the situation were put aside in the process of writing. He would study my representation of the facts, see immediately what needed to be done, and take action.

A week-and-a-half after receiving my letter, McKee phoned to report a lack of progress. He had put one of his assistants to work phoning directory assistance in Portland, Oregon, in search of David Sumner, even though I told him in my statement of our own dead-end efforts. He had also managed, somehow, to overlook Sumner's listing of David Jones as an alternative name. When we pointed this out, he replicated our fruitless phone calls in search of Mr. Jones, probably turning up Joneses Sr. and Jr. again and adding to whatever puzzlement and pleasure they took in Nancy's original misdirected queries. Though I realize that lawyers double-check information provided by their clients, it was frustrating to find McKee wandering down the cul de sacs we had clearly marked for him with No Exit signs.

A month of silence ensued, and when I next contacted McKee, I found him almost as uninterested in the case as at the outset. The search for a telephone listing had gone nowhere, so he simply stopped and was awaiting instructions from me, which was disheartening and eroded my image of him as a take-charge guy. I reminded him we had a valid mailing address that might lead to Sumner. After all, didn't lawyers have access to "reverse" phone directories, those organized by addresses rather than names, or was that simply a movie convention?

McKee's next move, in response to my prodding, was

in fact movie-like. He hired a Portland private investigator, Anne Bunch, who located David Sumner, discovered that his real name was David Jones, and provided McKee with his phone number, listed in his wife's name, seemingly in less time than it took McKee to ride the elevator to his office where her fax awaited him. Eager to confront Sumner/Jones directly, McKee now had access to him, and when he phoned the number, he turned on his tape machine. We later obtained a copy of this recording, along with a second one of a follow-up call, and it plays like something out of Samuel Beckett or Neil Simon (depending on my mood when I listen)—absurd, farcical, the sound of a man manipulated by a pro.

The call begins with McKee, sounding nervous, asking if he has reached David Sumner. When the reply is "Yes," McKee identifies himself and sets forth the reason for his call: "I represent Neal Bowers, who is a poet, and he asked me to bring to your attention, which I think you are aware of, the fact that you have copied poems of his and had them published." "No," is the incredulous response. After some hesitation, McKee then tries to determine if Sumner writes poetry ("No," again) and, finally, asks if he lives at the Aloha address known to be Sumner/Jones's. A final, "No," from Sumner/Jones is followed by an address in the Portland suburb of Milwaukie and then silence. He simply holds the line until McKee finally excuses himself, apologizing for having disturbed this innocent man. The two of them actually say "Bye-bye" to one another in a bizarre kind of kidspeak.

McKee's performance strikes me as the verbal equivalent of a man in a bumper car. Bearing down on his target, he suddenly loses control of his steering, bounces off the rail a couple of times, and comes to a standstill. The fact that Sumner/Jones placed him in that crazy rink when McKee assumed himself to be driving down an ordinary highway is only mildly mitigating. Nor was Anne Bunch amused later when McKee asked her to check the accuracy of her information. Obviously feeling that her professional integrity had been called into doubt, she hammered him with evidence of Jones's identity, everything from his driver's license to his voter registration. She also checked out the Milwaukie address claimed by the person McKee spoke with and discovered it did not exist. Her conclusion, in short, was that McKee had spoken with David Sumner/Jones and been deceived.

What is most striking about McKee's initial phone encounter with Sumner/Jones is the latter's coolness. Undoubtedly taken by surprise when McKee called, he wasn't quick enough to deny the name David Sumner, but he recovered in time to invent an address and claim he was another David Sumner. Right name, wrong guy and wrong town. Sorry. He volunteered nothing else, expressed no interest in the reason for McKee's call, and left my lawyer to fill the silences on the line between Iowa and Oregon. He had the attributes of an excellent trial witness, answering simply yes and no.

Thank God for Anne Bunch, whose secret weapon is a mild manner that disguises her savvy approach and gritty determination. She confided to Nancy that people willingly give her any kind of information she seeks —we assume because she doesn't threaten them. Like almost every woman who became involved in this case, Anne Bunch immediately recognized Sumner/Jones as a "wrong guy." She understood from the beginning what kind of person she was investigating; and it plainly distressed her when the lawyer who sent her to find Sumner/Jones believed him rather than her. Near the end of her faxed letter substantiating her original discoveries, she suggested to McKee (with sweet irony), "Perhaps the gentleman that you reached was not being honest with you."

So thorough was Anne Bunch's substantiation of Sumner/Jones's identity that she even found out what model car he drove and who held the lien on it. But the pièce de resistance of her work came in a conversation with the manager of the apartment complex where Sumner/Jones lived with his wife and young daughter. Asked if David Jones had a work number on file, the manager responded, "No, he works at home as a writer." This was evidence even Bruce McKee could accept as definitive. Should he require more, Anne Bunch stood ready to provide it, no doubt; and I am confident she could have discovered whether Jones wears boxer shorts or briefs, if the detail had seemed relevant.

Because McKee left on an out-of-state trip immediately after his phone call to Sumner/Jones, he delegated the job of contacting Bunch to one of his assistants and was not in the office when her follow-up confirmation arrived. Sitting here in Ames, thirty-five miles north of McKee's law office, we didn't know any of this was going on. So when the following letter bearing a Japanese postmark arrived, we had no idea what had prompted it:

Dear Mr. Neal Bowers,

I recently received an urgent call from my brother after he received a call of inquiry regarding poetry written by a poet, David Sumner. The caller—whom [sic] has received several calls in the past that were for me—said that you had called him asking about a poet. In any case, he contacted my brother to see if he knew whether I knew anything about the matter. The information presented was that a poem by Mr. Neal Bowers—with death as its theme—had been submitted, by David Sumner, and accepted. After hearing the information, I realized that I *had* submitted a poem entitled, "Aspects of Death," to several journals in 1990 or 1991, and it had been accepted for publication by *Seneca Review* out of New York and *San Jose Studies* from California. If this is your poem, Mr. Bowers, I am sorry for presenting it as my own. In the last poetry workshop I attended, the format was that on Monday we placed our typed poem(s) or a good photocopy in the professor's basket on the wall beside his office door. On Tuesday we picked up a packet of collected poems—some of which were poems written by professional poets, a few of his own, and some of ours—without titles or the poet's name appearing on the work. The workshop format was supposed to try and develop a critical eye and ear to help us distinguish between excellent and mediocre poetry. During the week (on our own) we evaluated each poem—not knowing who the poet was—and tried to determine what specifics made one poem superior to another. After our individual critique and round-table discussion of the work, the instructor told us the poet's name. At the end of the workshop, I had probably two hundred poems—most of which had the poet's name affixed but some that did not. As part of the evaluation process, we were asked to generate a name or names that would be appropriate for the piece and sight [sic] any questions regarding changes in syntax that we thought would strengthen the piece. The poem personifying death moved me the most of any during the course. I have read it and recited it many times since and now I find out that I also took it to be my own—when it was not. And now I find out that it is yours, Mr. Bowers. I apologize for any hurt that I have brought to you, your colleagues, and family. I am sorry. I do remember that the instructor—mentioned above—said that you and Seamus Heaney were his favorite poets. And now I find that in my conscious and unconscious you also reside as mine.

I have quit submitting poetry for publication—I don't have the money or the time—and now after this, I won't have the confidence. And this letter is a feeble attempt to apologize to you for embracing and proliferating your genius as my own.

I do remember that I submitted some poems to you at the *Poet and Critic* a couple of years ago, and that you took the time to send me a handwritten rejection slip . . . and now I commit this unconscious injustice against you after you showed me such kindness. Again, I send my apology to you, Mr. Bowers.

At my place of employment, I receive room and board and a small stipend. Last year—as disclosed on my tax statement—I earned $650.00. As recompense to you for my transgression, your trouble, and phone call, I have enclosed a money order payable to you.

I am sorry, Mr. Bowers. I meant you no harm.

> Sincerely,
> David Sumner
> Encl: bank draft

The return address was the same one passed along by the editors of *Half Tones to Jubilee* and *Hawaii Review,* so I already knew it was not valid. But the postage cancellation was real enough, and the envelope came from Japan. Sealed so securely with clear packaging tape as to defy opening, it might have been a letter bomb for all I knew.

If the contents weren't explosive, they were certainly

confounding. I had made no phone calls to locate Sumner and had no idea what unnamed person had telephoned Sumner's brother. Eventually, we would understand that Sumner was keeping up the ruse he used with McKee in combination with the Japanese deception. The two lies were blended in the following way: David Jones, pretending to be his alter ego David Sumner, living in Japan, claimed his brother received phone calls, presumably from the wrong "David Sumner," the one McKee had contacted. Wishing not to be bothered by any more phone calls about stolen poems, this "innocent" David Sumner somehow knew of the other David Sumner's existence and even had the wherewithal to discover and phone his brother. The brother, in turn, contacted the writer of this letter, who seemed to be the David Sumner I was looking for, and who was writing to me to clarify his situation.

Of course, clarity is not the intent of Sumner/Jones's letter, and his opening statements remind me of nothing so much as the classic "Who's on first" routine perfected by Abbott and Costello. The letter conspicuously omits any reference to McKee and credits me with having made McKee's "misdirected" phone call. By ignoring my attorney's existence, Sumner apparently hoped to put things on a purely personal level, appeasing me with an account of his "innocent" acquisition of my poetry and even apologizing. To make sure I would be placated, he enclosed a $100 money order (issued by an Oregon bank, which seemed odd, since Sumner was supposed to be in Japan).

In the way that certain poisonous molds and fungi can be beautiful, this letter is a lovely thing. The Japanese postmark discouraged further pursuit of David Sumner even before the contents of the envelope were known. The tape, we would later learn, was to prevent Sumner/

Jones's confederate in Japan (someone who owed him money, he confided, and would therefore help him out) from examining the contents before dropping the letter into the Japanese postal system. Inside, for me, was a harvest of numbing spores: apologies, excuses, flattery, and a little money. Not exactly the seven deadly sins but some of their cousins, once-removed.

Everything about the letter is excessive, particularly the whining pity patter and the linking of me and Seamus Heaney (though I don't know why he stopped short of Yeats once he got the idea to feed me my sweet self). Sumner/Jones's strategy was the same one used by my brother when we wrestled as kids. Four years older and quite a bit bigger, I could always subdue him, but he learned if he started kissing me, or even pretending to kiss me, I would run away in disgust. Sumner was planting sloppy smooches all over me.

Psychologically the letter is masterfully manipulative, but the best part is the explanation of how my poem came to have Sumner's name attached to it. His statement that he "took it to be my own" is wonderfully ambiguous, in one sense downright honest, as if he slipped when he meant to say "mistook it." The story accounts for how my poem may have come into his possession, how he may not have known the name of its true author, and why its title and smaller details were altered; but it does not explain how anyone could believe he wrote someone else's poem. All of us wish, from time to time, we had written something we admire, though few of us are delusional enough to assume ownership. Considering the autobiographical nature of "RSVP," assumption of authorship would require a degree of empathy bordering on obsession or schizophrenia.

For all it says, this letter is even more interesting for what it does not say. Nowhere does Sumner/Jones admit to plagiarism or accept responsibility for his actions, choosing instead to refer to an "unconscious injustice." Significantly, he muddles the ownership of the poem in question, apologizing in the subjunctive, "If this is your poem . . . I am sorry for presenting it as my own," and then later saying "now I find out that it is yours." While he mentions *Seneca Review* and *San Jose Studies,* he omits the other periodicals in which he published "RSVP" as his own and does not acknowledge Mark Strand's poem, even though the editors of *Half Tones to Jubilee* had long since confronted him. Most revealing is his failure to cite "Tenth-Year Elegy," that other poem of mine which he also "took to be his own" and published more than once.

Anne Bunch immediately offered to go right up to Sumner/Jones's door in Aloha and knock, if McKee wanted her personally to verify his identity and his presence there. Instead McKee chose to make a second phone call, one in which he sounded (as the second tape indicates) more assertive and sure of himself. At first Jones pretended he had never spoken with McKee before, but was then forced to concede his identity as McKee pressed harder with the facts, saying he was certain he was talking with the right person and recognized Jones's voice from his first call.

This conversation lasted thirty-five minutes and runs ten pages in typescript. Why Jones didn't simply hang up and refuse to be cornered is mysterious. Perhaps he thought he could brazen it out and escape McKee once more, or maybe he was actually exhilarated by the capture. Whatever the explanation, he held the line while McKee interrogated him. At no time during their exchange, however, did Jones actually admit he had plagiarized poetry. The closest he came was a stammering, breathless exclamation: "I'm . . . I'm very sorry, uh, of anything that, uh, was printed that wasn't mine. I'm, uh . . . I'm bewildered and I'm very sorry to Mr. Bowers or Mr. Strand." Assuming he had delivered a knockout blow, McKee said, "Well . . . " Whereupon Jones blurted, "And I promise, um, I have . . . basically I haven't worked in four and a half years and, uh, you know I'm just in very bad shape and I'm . . . I'm very sorry in [sic] Mr. Bowers and Mr. Strand and I . . . I promise I will never publish anything again or even try if . . . if, uh, you know even . . . I'm just very sorry, sir." Pressing hard, McKee cited the criminal code, "Section 2319, Criminal Infringement of a Copyright," and warned Jones he could be fined "up to $25,000 and . . . imprisoned for not more than one year or both." To avoid these dire consequences, McKee suggested Jones provide him with "something . . . that is convincing, that, you know, that you really mean what you say. And if you can write me a letter, you know, to that effect, I will take it to him and, you know, hopefully we can, we can end this."

Jones agreed to provide "something," though he couldn't have known what because McKee had presented no clear notion of the document he expected Jones to produce. Would it be a simple apology, an admission of guilt, a full disclosure of the extent of his plagiarisms, an offer of restitution? Seizing the vagueness of the moment, Jones began talking over McKee, edging him out, agreeing to do what he asked. Requesting McKee's mailing address, he slowly wrote it out, repeating each part and even asking how to spell my first name. No longer woozy, Jones was regaining control of the situation.

McKee then shifted into a more confidential mode, asking Jones to explain why he stole my poems. This part of the exchange plays like the resolution of a stock murder mystery. Trapped by the relentlessly cagey detective, the villain realizes the game is up and confesses everything. At least that's what McKee apparently thought was happening. In reality, Jones duplicated the workshop excuse he used in his "Japanese" letter, saying, "through the years . . . I basically thought that they were pieces I did." Nancy and I later discovered that he first submitted "Tenth-Year Elegy" as his own work within one month of my original publication of it in *Poetry*. Hardly enough time for the process of identification and assimilation Jones offered as his rationale.

In response to this explanation, McKee pressed for more personal information and learned that Jones was an unemployed teacher. When asked why he didn't have a job, Jones said, "Well, it's kind of a long story. It's hard to find work in my area." He further revealed that his wife was a public school teacher whose income supported the family. Mingled with these scant details were redundant apologies and a promise to send a letter that would somehow pacify me and persuade me not to press charges. McKee's only instructions to Jones were to write something that would "you know . . . make him believe that you're, you know . . . that you're committed to doing this." The meaning of "this" was never specified.

When McKee phoned to say he had contacted Sumner/Jones he was buoyant. "He'll do anything we ask," he said; "he's totally contrite and sorry." He described Jones as subdued and clearly regarded him as a beaten man. Caught up by McKee's enthusiasm, we felt relieved. To know Sumner/Jones had been made to respond to direct evidence of his plagiarisms was gratifying. It was troubling, however, to learn that Jones had explained himself to McKee in exactly the same way he had excused himself in the letter posted in Japan. Not to worry, McKee seemed to say, "He's faxing a letter tomorrow."

What came through via McKee's fax machine was a statement cobbled from pieces of the Japan letter, suggesting Jones was working with a boilerplate. The only new material it contained was the following:

> After receiving my Master of Arts degree in 1987, I started work on a novel. From then until now I have revised the work many times. After submitting many queries and sample chapters, I have still not been able to sell the work. In the interim, I have been a cook in a restaurant for six months, done a week's editing of a chapbook, and recently finished three weeks of writing assessment of high school students' creative writing papers. My points are that I do understand the devotion it takes to create art and that money—since I began writing seriously—has been nonexistent for me. Last year—as disclosed on my tax statement—I earned $650.00. As recompense to you for my wrongs against you, your trouble, and phone calls, I have mailed a money order for $100.00 payable to you, to your editorial office for the *Poet & Critic,* and I am mailing another money order for $100.00 to your lawyer's office in Des Moines, also in your name.
>
> I am sorry, Mr. Bowers.
>
> > Sincerely,
> > David Jones

McKee was entirely satisfied by this offering and couldn't understand why it seemed inadequate and incomplete to me. I looked at the letter for an admission of wrongdoing, for true contrition; and I also wanted an accounting of Jones's use of my poems. He had still not acknowledged stealing "Tenth-Year Elegy," and I knew from my correspondence with various editors that he lied when he said he had not submitted or published anything in over six months.

I tried to explain these things to McKee, but I'm sure he regarded me as an unreasonable puritan. The centerpiece of the letter, and the part probably of most interest to McKee, was the personal paragraph detailing years of unemployment. This man had no money; therefore, he was what the legal profession terms "judgment proof." Taken to court and found guilty, he could not pay any judgment assessed against him. Better to take what was offered, however unsatisfactory it might seem, and be done with this business. That appeared to be McKee's view.

Looking at Sumner/Jones, McKee saw no monetary reason for either of us to chase him into a court of law, and he advised me to clarify for myself what I really wanted to obtain through the legal system. "Justice" would have been my simple response, but it sounded almost stupidly idealistic in the context of such a pragmatic accounting. I had hired McKee out of desperation, hoping he could find Sumner/Jones and make him give back what he took from me. Of course, that was impossible. Those poems could never be wholly returned.

4.

A Law Against It

Recognizing my dilemma, McKee suggested I state exactly what I expected from Jones. He called this "a list of affirmative acts," which seemed a remarkably conciliatory phrase. Given the choice, I would have opted for "an itemized admission of guilt." Perhaps McKee felt I would discover, in the process of writing, that I already had everything I needed or wanted or could reasonably expect from Jones. As I compiled the list, I examined Jones's letter and became convinced I had to extract from him an unambiguous admission and a specific revelation of his activities as a plagiarist. If he was as wobbly on his feet as McKee said he was after their phone conversation, he might provide at least some of the information I requested. Most important to me was clarification of the bibliographic record. I didn't want it assumed, at some point in the future, that Sumner/Jones was the original author of my poems and I the plagiarist.

My demands were straightforward and not onerous, I thought; and I made them as particular as I could:

1. Mr. Jones should compile a list of all the journals to which he has submitted any poems since September 1990. The list should include titles, addresses, and names of editors.
2. Mr. Jones should send a letter of retraction to all journals which are currently considering his plagiarisms of "Tenth-Year Elegy" and "RSVP." The poems should be identified as plagiarisms and withdrawn. Copies of these letters should be forwarded to me as soon as the originals have been sent.
3. Mr. Jones should inform (by letter) editors who have published or accepted for publication plagiarisms of "Tenth-Year Elegy" and "RSVP" that they have published or accepted stolen work. Mr. Jones should identify me as the rightful author of those poems originally written by me and should send me copies of all the letters once he has mailed the originals.
4. Mr. Jones should identify by name and affiliation (i.e., university or workshop) the writing instructor in whose class Mr. Jones allegedly encountered my poems. A mailing address and phone number should also be provided for this person.
5. Mr. Jones should sign the attached statement acknowledging his plagiarisms of my work:

To Whom It May Concern:

I David Jones, also known as David Sumner, have plagiarized work by Neal Bowers and represented it as my own. Specifically, "Tenth-Year Elegy" and "RSVP," original poems by Neal Bowers, have been offered for publication and published by me with different titles under the name David Sumner.

Both "Tenth-Year Elegy" and "RSVP" were first published in the September 1990 issue of *Poetry* by Neal Bowers and are his sole property. All subsequent publications of these two poems by me under such variant titles as "Someone Forgotten," "My Careless Father," "Forgetfulness," "Aspects of Death," and any other titles were plagiarisms.

I make this statement of my own free will and sign my legal name below in the presence of a notary public.

Being obliged to state precisely what I wanted from Sumner/Jones helped me. Revenge was not on my agenda, nor had I imagined some settlement with Jones that would allow me to splash away my remaining years at Saint-Tropez. I simply wanted him to admit what he had done (and was still doing, we came to discover) and to set the record straight. An apology without an acknowledgment of responsibility was an empty gift box. If Jones were truly sorry and eager to make things right, he should be willing to disclose everything, which I considered unlikely, even though McKee insisted we could get whatever we wanted from him. Reviewing my list of requested "acts," McKee said emphatically, "He'll give us this information and sign the statement; don't worry." Despite misgivings, I felt better about my circumstances than at any time since discovering Jones garbed in my wardrobe.

Within a week of composing my list and forwarding it to McKee, I received the following letter from David Jones:

Dear Mr. Bowers,

I am sorry for all that I have done against you. In a perfect world, an artist like you—a creator of beauty—should never have to come in contact with such an ugliness as me.

Thank you for the humanity you have extended to me in this matter.

I have made my best attempt to fulfill the requests made by you and Mr. McKee.

I am sorry for distracting you from your work and life.

Sincerely,

David Jones

Reading this pathetic note, I saw why McKee felt Jones would do anything we asked. His obsequiousness made me feel I had robbed him of his last particle of dignity, and I was almost ashamed to have pushed so hard in defense of my work. At the same time, his abasement seemed exaggerated, and the note could be read as tongue-in-cheek hyperbole.

Trailing this strange note by three weeks, a box from Sumner/Jones was delivered to McKee's office, where Nancy and I examined its contents one June afternoon. Too heavy to be empty, it might have been filled with old newspapers, for all we knew, so we opened it with apprehension. Inside were stacks of papers and envelopes, all neatly arranged as if for permanent storage in some library's archives. A letter from Jones atop the materials detailed what he obviously wanted us to see as his good faith effort to comply with my demands, but it began with a limiting provision: "After days of searching through drawers and boxes—in a storage room and a friend's garage (our two bedroom apartment has only 850 square feet), I have found the material I have."

Cramped and redundant, he cried out, I have what I have. No one could argue that point, but the subsequent text made it clear Jones had not supplied us with complete documentation of his activities. The letter described slip-shod record keeping. Saying he "did not keep a submissions log citing specific poems by name that were submitted to certain journals," he claimed he noted only the date of submission in the margin beside each periodical's listing in *Poet's Market.* Such haphazard management could work only for someone unconcerned about multiple submissions and publications, someone like Jones, who sent "My Father," his theft of "Tenth-Year Elegy," to the *same* periodical that had accepted it only four months earlier as "Someone Forgotten."

Jones described his efforts to identify all the periodicals to which my poems had been sent: "If any publications are omitted in this process, it is because I believe that the submission has already been rejected by the editor(s), not because of any nefarious act." This disclaimer seems to account for the possibility that we would discover other plagiarisms. In fact, we kept secret our knowledge of several, to use as a check on the completeness of the materials he provided. If he disclosed only those he knew we were aware of, his documents could not be trusted.

Boxed beneath this letter were the following items: (1) photocopies of letters from six editors accepting one or both of my poems as submitted by Jones posing as David Sumner, and sealed letters of retraction ready for mailing to them; (2) a list of four workshops Jones claimed to have attended; (3) a 64-page file labeled "Poems," including my two on top; (4) two "sample" covering letters Jones mailed with his poetry submissions, each containing information for a contributor's note; (5) a list of 44 periodicals to which

Jones claimed he had submitted work; (6) sealed envelopes addressed to 47 periodicals, including the 44 on the list; and (7) a single photocopied page from *Poet's Market* to illustrate Jones's record-keeping, such as it was.

At a glance Sumner/Jones seemed to have done his best to comply with the first four of my five affirmative acts. The only thing missing was his signed admission of responsibility. But there were troubling holes in the material as well. The biggest involved the list of six periodicals Jones claimed had accepted my poems under his name. While we were aware of several of them, we knew of four others that were not listed, and we would ultimately learn of nine more. Similarly, the 64 pages of poetry, characterized by Jones as "various poems (all that I could dig up)," included only 10 known to be printed under the name David Sumner. Not included were the Strand plagiarism or others we eventually discovered stolen by Jones from Sharon Olds, Marcia Hurlow, and Robert Gibb. In the coming months, an additional 43 "Sumner" poems materialized, all published but none "dug up" by him.

The bulk of the poetry in Jones's box was bad. Nothing he actually published approached the inferiority of these manuscripts. Hackneyed and overwritten, they were the record of a failed poet or, more accurately, a failed effort to become a poet. Looking at them page by page, I tried to discern the labor and longing I saw in the juvenilia of poets who developed into notable writers, or even in the early work of my more successful students. Jones's creations showed no spark, no promise of better things to come.

As the omissions became obvious, we wondered what was in those 47 envelopes bound for an assortment of literary periodicals ranging from *Hudson Review* to *Mudfish*.

We opened the one addressed to our good friend George Core, editor of the *Sewanee Review,* knowing George wouldn't mind, would even be amused to know we had selected him for our random test, and had found the following:

> Editor,
>
> If you have not already rejected my poetry submission to you, would you please do so and discard the work. It has been discovered that I have presented the poetry genius of another poet as my own. To comply with the poet's request, I am contacting any editor, to whom I have submitted work, to request that the poems that I have submitted be discarded. I apologize for my betrayal of the trust that you, as an editor, place in those poets who submit work to you. I am sorry for any problems that I have caused you and your associates. Because I value the art of great poetry, I will never submit poetry to you again. I apologize for having to use a photocopy to contact you.
>
> Sincerely,
David Sumner

The conspicuous absence of my name as the poet whose work was stolen leaves open the possibility Jones meant to cover all the poets whom he had copied into his own oeuvre. But the passive voice—"It has been discovered that . . . "—gives the whole statement a vague quality and enables Jones to avoid accepting full responsibility for his thefts, like the company spokesman who intones, "Mistakes were made" when the employees' retirement fund is missing. Not exactly a brilliant bit of rhetoric, but the best strategy was invisible and wouldn't become apparent for several weeks, when a spot-check of editors to whom Jones sent this letter revealed none had anything from him under consideration, and their logbooks contained neither of his names.

Although I did not contact all 47 editors, I feel certain each was puzzled to receive a quasi-admission of plagiarism and a retraction of work never submitted. Jones protected himself by signing his pseudonym, admitting to no particular instance of plagiarism, and then circulating his letter to periodicals with which he had transacted no business. Not one of the 42 periodicals (a number which is likely to grow as more discoveries are made) which actually accepted or published work he sent them was included in his list. Piece by piece, Jones's documents revealed he had fulfilled none of the affirmative acts.

Further pressure from McKee elicited only a claim that Jones had done his best to meet my demands, and he was particularly resistant to signing the statement of responsibility. Addressing this final item, Jones wrote:

> I have enclosed a statement that I would be willing to sign and have notarized. The statement that was enclosed is not reality, and if I signed it, it would open me up to civil and criminal suit by any representative of any journal to which I submitted the works in question and any journal in which the works have been published. I have done my best to cooperate in this matter, Mr. McKee, but some of these requests are impossible. By looking through the materials that I have enclosed in the box sent to you you can see that I have done a thorough job in my effort to comply with all your requests. Before I could sign the statement that I have forwarded to you via mail, I would have to have an original statement signed by Mr. Neal Bowers stating that he or any agent employed by him will not file civil or criminal suit

against me. I have worked hard to comply with the requests of you, Mr. McKee, and those of Mr. Bowers.

> Sincerely,
> David Jones
> Encl.: revised statement of responsibility

Jones's revision was longer than my statement because he appended to it his protracted rationale of receiving my poems in a workshop and coming to believe they were his own. The altered statement Jones was willing to sign was an excuse rather than an acceptance of responsibility. Even so, I might have tolerated it had he not insisted I waive any future lawsuit against him.

McKee was still certain we could get whatever concessions we wanted from Jones. He understood I could not sign any document relinquishing my rights to sue Jones, but he continued to believe he could get Jones to sign my original statement without capitulation by me. My feeling that there had been a change in the weather made me less sanguine. Jones now showed flashes of energy and determination; and in his defiance we thought we saw, for the first time, the real David Sumner/Jones.

Future looks at Jones would come only in glimpses; a phone call or two to McKee, a few postcards, and then nothing. Among his last communications was this letter to Nancy, dated two days after his revised statement of responsibility:

Dear Ms. Bowers,
I am sorry. I am the person who presented two of your husband's poems to literary journal editors as my own. After being contacted in this matter, and finding the works in *Poetry* magazine, and seeing that the poems were dedicated

to you, I was devastated even more. By my actions I have violated art devoted by the artist to the person of his inspiration. I have a wife and daughter and I love them very much; they inspire me every day. I know how important love and friendship is.

In a generalized appraisal of human behavior, I believe that most women are more forgiving and empathetic than men; I also believe that most men are driven by vengeance. I am doing all that I can to rectify the sad situation that I have thrust into your husband's life.

I am sorry to have sullied the art that your husband has created and devoted to you.

I will not sign this apology because I do not want you to focus on anything but the words.

Nancy dropped the sheet on the kitchen counter where she opened the envelope. For her, the voice on the page produced the same effect as an obscene phone call. She was frightened because Jones knew her name, and furious that he thought he could manipulate her to his advantage. His assessment of women as "more forgiving and empathetic than men" was not substantiated by our experience. Women saw him as despicable; whereas men were more likely to give him the benefit of the doubt. Even had that not been the case, Jones's hypothesis was so bound up in condescension it was loathsome. Apparently, Nancy was supposed to intercede with me on his behalf, simply because her "forgiving" nature would not permit her to do otherwise. Nancy was intimately involved in my efforts to find Jones and hold him accountable, but he had no way of knowing this or how badly he had misjudged her.

Also troubling was Jones's reference to poems dedi-

cated to Nancy. Neither of my poems known to be plagiarized and published repeatedly by Jones carries a dedi-
cation to her, although many others do, the majority of
them appearing in *Poetry*. Perhaps not exactly the same as
a mobster's threat—"You got a nice little family there. Be
a shame if something happened to 'em"—Jones's letter
resembled it enough to leave us feeling at risk. The ending, especially, sounded ominous: "I will not sign this
apology because I do not want you to focus on anything
but the words." Exactly how his signature would detract
isn't clear, but the implication that Nancy should pay very
careful attention to him suggests he wanted her to receive
a message other than the literal one. The practical effect of
omitting his signature was a confession he could subsequently deny. Although his address was typed on the
envelope, his name appeared nowhere on the correspondence, giving his admission of guilt as much value as the
unsigned statement of responsibility.

Through the veil of anonymity, we glimpsed the true
face of David Jones. Until now, he had relied upon David
Sumner, his fumbling, oily apologist; but Jones himself
stood ready to take charge if things got too complicated.
Nancy and I both sensed in this doubleness a treacherous
and potentially dangerous division of personality. Feeling
less secure ourselves, we couldn't shake the apprehension
that Sumner/Jones was capable of worse acts than stealing poems.

The most significant effect of this letter, for me, was the
permanent elimination of any doubts I had about Sum-
ner/Jones's culpability. Whatever explanation he might
offer, his activities betrayed a willful and sustained appropriation of other poets' works, primarily mine. For Nancy,
the letter consolidated all she had previously intuited

about Jones. Because he addressed her in a confidential, almost intimate way, she now took his activities more personally than before and became determined not to let him escape.

Jones, however, was already packing to depart. Responding to further efforts by McKee to have him sign the statement of responsibility, he said he couldn't attend to the matter immediately as he was driving to Illinois to visit his mother, who suffers from Alzheimer's disease. Sumner, the name of the town where she lived, resonated like a bad parody of W. C. Williams's city/man Paterson. Sumner the place, Sumner the man. He promised on his return he would work with McKee to resolve everything. As an article of good faith, he gave McKee his Illinois mailing address and a phone number where he could be reached at his brother's house. McKee later tried unsuccessfully to contact him there, although he did find his brother at home. Apart from the following odd postcard, mailed from Kankakee, Illinois, David Jones was no longer available:

Dear Mr. McKee,

In continuing to maintain contact with you, I want to inform you that I have not been able to reach my brother at his residence.

Upon my return to Oregon, I will send the letters to the editors in which the works have already been published.

Sincerely,
David Jones

Jones's promise to send letters to editors kept up the pretense of trying to comply with my requests. But the note was dated one month before it was postmarked, a discrepancy which may have been a slip of the pen, but which raises the possibility that Jones wrote and forwarded the postcard to a friend in Kankakee for mailing at a predetermined time. Why he could not locate his brother is only a little less puzzling than what became of his ill mother. As in all other interactions with Jones, the truth was a vaporous and shifting thing.

Having successfully faked living in Japan, Jones must have found it simple to pretend traveling in Illinois. Efforts to phone him when he was supposedly back in Aloha revealed that his number had been disconnected. And we later learned that he and his family moved from their apartment on a date coinciding with their "return" from the Midwest. Like the sleight-of-hand artist, Jones said, "Look over there!" and then vanished.

The possibility of his flight was not foremost when I thought of what Jones might do. In fact, I was more worried he would pass through Ames en route to Illinois, not for a confrontation but just to drive down our street and feel the voyeur's rush of secret control. Once he decamped from Aloha, I doubted we would find him without great difficulty. I was certain he wouldn't voluntarily contact us again, but after nearly two months of silence he sent me at my home address a certified envelope bearing the following letter among its contents:

Dear Mr. Bowers,

I have fulfilled all of your requests that are possible for me to accomplish. At the same time that I mail this letter to you, I am returning to the editors—via mail at book rate—the journals in which the poems that have been proven to me are really works by you [sic]. Therefore, I have received no payment for the poems—that are yours—published under my pseudonym. I have also enclosed a money order in your name for $400.00. This, combined with the two $100.00 checks already sent, totals $600.00. Last year I earned $650.00. I send this money as reparation for the trouble that I have caused you as a result of my accident of process.

I am sorry for any problems that I have caused you during this matter, but it was an accident, not a deliberate act.

> Sincerely,
> David Jones
> Encls.: money order, 2 letters,
> & a journals list

The list of 62 periodicals was another display of his "good faith" attempt to provide all requested information. Although it included many we had not known about, it was more notable, as was Jones's earlier accounting, for those omitted. One missing periodical was the *Laurel Review,* which published his theft of my "RSVP" under the title "Aspects of Death." Bill Trowbridge, one of the periodical's editors, later told me Jones phoned him prior to publication, claiming the poem had been published elsewhere and offering to withdraw it. Because the issue was already typeset, Trowbridge indicated he would publish it anyway, if there were no other problems with the poem. Jones said he could think of none.

A copy of the covering letter Jones claimed to have sent to all periodical editors on his list contained the familiar workshop rationale and ended with this statement:

In agreement with the poet whom I have wronged and because I value the art of great poetry, I will never again submit poetry for publication to you or any other editor. I have enclosed the journal(s) that you paid to me for allowing you to publish a poem that I believed was my own.

The envelope containing these materials bore Jones's defunct address but was postmarked in Tualatin, another Portland suburb. Perhaps he simply moved across town, or maybe he prevailed on yet another friend to drop mail. Whatever the case, he was no longer accessible, and we later learned that his wife resigned her teaching position and took a job in a U.S. military school in Germany. Presumably, David went with her.

Between McKee's first phone call to Jones and Jones's final letter to me, a little less than five months elapsed. During that time, he manufactured so much misleading information and told so many outright lies that some aspects of the story are obscure even to me. I grew to doubt everything he said, although his fictions were sometimes accreted around grains of truth. He did have a brother in Illinois, for instance, but he almost certainly did not visit him. As for the ailing mother, she may have been dead for years, according to the unpublished manuscripts Jones included in his box of materials. But he vanished so efficiently, it is possible to wonder if Sumner/Jones ever existed in either of his incarnations.

Turning to McKee for the help I still hoped he would provide, I wrote to inquire if criminal action against Jones for mail fraud was possible and requested information about the approximate costs of a civil suit. As candidly as I could, I sought "frank and direct guidance" and, in particular, McKee's expert opinion of the "best possible outcome" of my pursuit of Jones and "specific ways to arrive at it." He never responded to these queries and, instead, presented a bill for his services: $4,155.37. When I requested an itemized statement, McKee provided a record of "billable hours." Among items for which we were charged at $200 per hour was a chance encounter with McKee on the day we examined Jones's box of materials. Our curiosity led McKee's secretary to show us his office, which occupies a corner of the thirty-seventh floor of Des Moines' tallest building, giving a panoramic view of the compact downtown area and the suburbs trailing off into corn and soybean fields. Just as we stepped into the room, McKee returned from a meeting, passed a few pleasantries while showing us his artwork, and then billed us for a 15-minute consultation. I protested this and other billable items but received no reply from McKee.

To be fair, I should say McKee accomplished some things, considering how little he initially believed in my case and how uninterested he seemed in its details. Perhaps we were destined to misunderstand one another. The poet seeking some kind of justice and the attorney accustomed to the legalities of patents certainly made an odd couple. As if to symbolize our failure of communication, enclosed with McKee's bill was a photocopy of the copyright laws supposedly relevant to my case. They were the laws governing the reproduction of sound recordings.

Possibly, no attorney would have had better luck grappling with Sumner/Jones. McKee at least got Jones's attention and a good amount of incomplete documentation, although he never obtained the single thing I wanted most: a signed admission of Jones's responsibility and his acknowledgment that my poems were my poems. But for the skill and determination of Anne Bunch, whom McKee had the good fortune to employ briefly, we might never have located Jones.

5.

A Method in It

BECAUSE THE hero is measured by the stature of his nemesis, I wished for David Jones to be brilliant, a cynical genius who could have done wonderful things had he chosen to but who, for whatever reasons, had gone wrong. Whenever anyone asked about him, I emphasized his mystery, stressing how little we knew about him, giving him an aura of worthiness. If you're going to have your wallet lifted, better to have it done by Light Fingers Freddie, known from Picadilly to Petaluma for his classic style, not by some bungler in need of a fix who tears your pocket and knocks you over during the procedure.

Finesse was not Jones's trademark, however. His was a more in-your-face approach. Perhaps he was like the protester who jumps the fence at the missile site and forces his arrest to make a point. Plagiarism as civil disobedience, now there was a novel idea. Secretly I hoped Jones was out to make some kind of point about the literary marketplace and the condition of American poetry. Perhaps he wanted to show how attention to writing has been displaced by a focus on publishing, how nobody seems to read anyway.

Imagining Jones engaged in plagiarism for principled reasons was a little like crediting the termite for carpentry; but like my mother-in-law, who can make up an entire life-history for someone she observes in line at the supermarket, I was creating an identity and a purpose for Jones. No difference between my fiction for the poetry thief and hers for "the lonely man with three cans of tuna and a loaf of bread in his cart, a recent widower, probably, just trying to get by." In fact, lacking an opportunity for personal observation of my subject, I had less evidence upon which to base any speculations than she ever did. The closest I had come was hearing Jones's voice on McKee's tape recordings.

Nancy had said he sounded creepy. He repulsed me, too, but I got the clear sense from hearing him try to evade and then manipulate McKee that he was probably much more intelligent than he sounded. Not being forthcoming was a strategy rather than the manifestation of a dull mind. Also evident in his voice was the edgy tone of the bluffer, especially when he capitulated during the second call and admitted he and David Sumner were indeed the same person. We had expected Jones to sound Irish or English, because he claimed a British Isles heritage in his contributor's notes. Instead he came through as a disembodied voice in search of an identity.

The ordinary plagiarist publishes his stolen goods under his true name because he wants to be given credit for them, possession being the immediate objective of stealing. But Jones's persona of David Sumner distanced him from his actions, making the convention of the nom de plume more a criminal front than a literary pose. The things he chose to say about himself in his contributor's notes were, of course, suspect. At the outset, though, they constituted all the information we had about him, affording the following profile:

> David Sumner was born in Ireland and lived in England until age 11. He received his B.A. degree in English from Southern Illinois University, where he studied medieval literature with Edmund Epstein and creative writing with John Gardner. He received his M.A. in English from Pacific University and also studied with William Stafford in the Haystack Program.

In addition to these biographical details, Jones always cited three or four periodicals where Sumner's poems had appeared or were forthcoming. However, none of these "facts" stood up. A check with the English Department at Southern Illinois University failed to confirm he had been one of their majors, although he did receive a baccalaureate degree in 1975, in elementary education. Because John Gardner is dead, we were unable to verify that Sumner/Jones had been a student of his. William Stafford could find no evidence of Sumner/Jones ever having studied with him. As for the M.A. in English from Pacific University, it turned out to be a master of arts in teaching degree with an emphasis in English. Even some of the periodical credits proved false, although many of them provided valuable leads and enabled me to intercept poems of mine before they were published as David Sumner's.

To consider just these items, Sumner appears to be a modified Jones, his credentials slightly altered to give them a little more polish. The best lies are always founded on elements of the truth, a strategy Jones used to perfection. His occasional use of other pseudonyms is more puzzling: David Johns (adopted, he said, when he attended workshops), David Ahlstrom (derived from his wife's maiden name), David Summer (possibly a typographical error), David Compton, and, most intriguing of all, Diane Compton. The latter name was used several times and was attached to two poems in the Spring/Summer 1992 issue of *Whiskey Island Magazine,* which also included David Sumner's plagiarism of my "RSVP." Thus, a single magazine fell for two of Jones's false identities. The contributor's note for Diane Compton appeared as follows:

> Diane Compton, former co-editor of the now defunct *Margin* literary journal of Glasgow, Scotland, earned her M.A. degree at the University of Oregon. She studied poetry with Philip Levine at Fresno State College and with Louise Gluck in the Warren Wilson Residency Program. Her work has appeared in *Tenth Decade, Salmagundi, London Review of Books,* and many others. She lives in Aloha, Oregon.

Ruth Young, co-editor of *Primavera,* received submissions from both Sumner and Compton and noticed they had the same return address. Closer inspection revealed that their cover letters and envelopes were typed on the same machine and that both signatures were made by the same hand using the same pen. We later discovered that poems sometimes circulated under the name Diane Compton were also submitted under the name David Sumner.

Jones's creation of a persona different from himself in gender and background raises the possibility that he used other names and concocted other biographies still to be discovered. Apart from David Sumner, his other known aliases have not been found attached to poems, although Jones's listing of them on his change of address card when he left Aloha, Oregon, and arranged to have his mail forwarded suggests that manuscripts bearing those names were circulating to editors. Clearly he wanted to keep track of "his" submissions even while evading me and my charges. Maintaining an up-to-date log of his poetic activity would have been a full-time job, however.

Using *Poet's Market*, with its nearly 2,000 listings, Jones seems to have had an alphabetical approach to periodicals. From the "W's," he chose *The Wayne Literary Review, West Branch, Whiskey Island Magazine, The Windless Orchard, The Wise Woman, Writer's Forum,* and *Writer's Journal.* The "P's" afforded him *The Panhandler, The Piedmont Literary Review, Plainsong, Poet Lore, The Pointed Circle, The Portland Review, Poem, Primavera,* and *Protea.* All are periodicals in which he published.

While Jones was inclusive, he was also indiscriminate. Many of the periodicals to which he submitted were so obscure and ephemeral they were unobtainable beyond the locale of their production and many have ceased operation in the few years since Jones's peak activity. In the crowd are publications devoted to vampirism, beer, insomnia, juggling, mountain climbing, pipe-smoking, and insects. Virtually any topic can be found among the directory listings, along with statements of editorial preferences. The editor of *Insomnia & Poetry* advises, "We don't think poetic expression is some privilege to be 'crafted' by only a select bunch. We think of it as human expression that can be shown by anyone—a cathartic endeavor for all." *Experimental Basement*'s editor is happy to read poems written on "toilet paper, golf balls, matchbook covers—everything, really, as long as it's readable."

Recent issues of *A Directory of American Poets and Fiction Writers* list more than 7,000 authors. No one knows how many more are unlisted or what the total number of people regularly circulating poems to periodicals might be— enough to pack a good-sized gym, let's say. Somewhere on those bleachers, David Jones took a seat. To the editors he encountered he appeared polished and professional. In fact, he resembled nothing so much as the garden variety M.F.A. student, touting his credentials and recent publications in every cover letter and blanketing the country with his submissions. Easy to understand how he could hide in plain view and how any editor, even the most conscientious, could be taken in by him.

During my seven years as editor of the small literary magazine *Poet & Critic*, I read an average of 5,000 poems between September and May, the months most periodicals operate. Of all those submitted poems, I published approximately 20 in each of three issues, for a total of 60 per year, which made acceptance only a little less rare than the feats of levitation claimed to occur down the road at Maharishi International University. Keeping up with the unending arrival of manuscripts was nearly impossible. During the worst times, I felt as if I were bailing out a river with a bucket—so much brackish backwash and so few fish. No need to reflect on those poems handwritten on ring-binder paper or those beginning, "I don't know why / I want to die." Similarly, poems so worn from travel that they broke at their creases and any carrying a handwritten copyright symbol could be tossed aside.

The difficult decisions involved poems displaying a level of competence, probably acquired in a workshop but revealing no special qualities to set them apart from the other competent poems, plentiful as carp. Because I viewed the editor as someone who tries to help, I spent more time than was good for me attempting to coax originality out of these writers, sending them specific notes about their poems and compounding my workload by implicitly encouraging them to send back. Judging from David Jones's fond memories of my remarks on "his" submitted poems, I spent some time encouraging him as well. Perhaps I paused over the poems he sent because they stood out like a catch in the surrounding pool—as well they might, having probably already been landed by at least one other editor. Embarrassing to think I may have been reading plagiarized poems. Worse to think I may have come close to accepting and publishing one or two.

Any editor working earnestly through the flood of submissions on any given day would probably be tempted to haul in the poems Jones signed with his pseudonym. That he had my two poems accepted a total of 20 times is not surprising, and I don't take it as a personal compliment. More than anything, perhaps, it's a reflection of editorial desperation. Work doesn't have to be sensational and irresistible to call attention to itself; it simply has to be better than what slides by, minnowlike on the steady current, 99 percent of the time.

The best periodicals, receiving in excess of 60,000 poems per year, must be hated by their local postal workers. Although less than one percent of the total ever finds its way into print at these top publications, someone has to read (or attempt to read) everything. Boredom, exhaustion, and a certain amount of resistance are engendered in all poetry editors, but the truly gifted ones somehow retain their enthusiasm for the job. Unfortunately, I cannot count myself among them, because I became weary and cynical after only a single cycle of the locusts. Knowing what I know about the editorial business, I am not without empathy for those who stick with the labor.

Good and bad editors alike were vulnerable to Jones, as the acceptance letters included in Jones's box of materials reveal. Ruth Young, co-editor of *Primavera*, accepting Jones's version of my "Tenth-Year Elegy," wrote:

Dear David Sumner:

Thanks for sending your work to *Primavera*. Sorry it has taken so long to get back to you; with a move (note address above) some things were misplaced.

I—as a first reader—was very enthusiastic about "Father's Forgetfulness," but others of our group of co-editors had some problems with the opening of the first stanza. Through discussion, the consensus was to ask you to consider moving "Always leaving me at rest-stops, coffee shops / some wide spot in the road; / " to the top of the poem.

Also—and I agree with this one—a less prosy title would be nice.

I sincerely hope that we've not lost this poem; I'd love to see what you do with it.

Bizarre as it is to overhear my poem talked about as though it were written by someone else, it is gratifying to note how Ruth Young and her colleagues went directly to the parts of the poem Jones substantially altered, the title and first line, sensing them to be weak or inappropriate. In the plagiarism of Robert Gibb's poem "The Race," stolen from the same issue of *Poetry* as my work, the final two stanzas were deleted, perhaps because Jones failed to turn the page and find them printed on the reverse side. I like to think he was photocopying poems into his oeuvre and came up one coin short of completing the job.

Also accepting Jones's plagiarism of "Tenth-Year Elegy," Kathryn Van Spanckeren, poetry editor of *Tampa Review*, had no reservations whatsoever:

> Dear David Sumner:
>
> I am happy to tell you that we at *Tampa Review* are taking "Father's Forgetfulness" and "Language." The contract is being sent under separate cover.
>
> Both the poems were excellent in their feeling and language and we are looking forward to seeing them in our magazine. You should know that the editors were unanimous in liking your poems—something rare with us. The poems seemed vivid and unforced, and fresh.
>
> Thank you for sending us your fine work.

Over and over, David Jones found the trusting editors of poetry periodicals easy marks. And his deception was enabled by those editors who were indifferent to his activities. Kelly Sarsano, for example, responding to my warning that Jones was listing her magazine, *The Sandhills Review*, among his credits, reported that a quick check turned up no poems by Sumner in the recent past and said a more extensive search of back issues would be a waste of her time: "We cannot check at this point in time and would not gain a thing by finding out." Evelyn J. Miles, managing editor of *Piedmont Literary Review*, acknowledged her periodical's publication of Sumner's theft of my "Tenth-Year Elegy" and went on to say, "I only wish that this type of thing could somehow be stopped, but as you know, it is impossible. Best of luck in your prosecution of this case!"

Rachel Stevens, editor of *The Pointed Circle*, confessed to feeling "particular dismay" at having published my stolen poem and then said, "Thank you for alerting us to this problem." Despite her good intentions, she gave no indication she would run an editorial statement and closed her letter by asking for "any suggestions you might have for avoiding such problems in the future." Then there was Gunvor Skogsholm, editor of *Poetry Forum*, who chastised me for lacking sufficient humility to keep quiet:

> It's my strongly felt opinion that a good poet by nature ought to possess humbleness and that he or she ought not to think to [sic] highly of him- or herself. Throughout history, those have always been the personal traits associated with a POET. If you have read any of the literary histories associated with the great names in the art of poetry, you will know this is so.

As distressing and occasionally offensive as these and similar responses were, they at least constituted replies to my warnings and requests for information. A large number of editors never responded, including many who published my poems under the name David Sumner. Of course, they may have declined to respond on the chance I might be lying or suffering delusions of persecution; and even if I were telling the truth, my news made me unwelcome because it complicated their lives.

Oddest of all were editors who initially showed interest in my predicament and then backed away. Several even contacted me on their own, pledging assistance and then withdrawing when I responded. Others fled from me while implying I was the problem. Such was the case in Portland, Oregon, where Sumner / Jones had been published and poetry readings set up for him. Milla Walker, of the Portland Poetry Festival, and Max Provino, co-editor of *The Portland Review,* phoned to express dismay and offer whatever help they could but then failed to return my calls or answer my letters. I gave up hope of receiving any support from them when one of the festival committee members let me know that he regarded my predicament as nothing more than a "poetry snit."

Roberta George, of *Snake Nation Review,* suggested that I somehow staged the whole affair. Referring to Jones's letter of retraction, one of six included in his box of partial disclosures, she noted, "We received an admission of guilt and an apology from David Sumner, return address Aloha, OR, but postage validation says Des Moines, IA." Because my letters, too, bear a Des Moines cancellation, the implication was inescapable. I didn't bother to tell her that Jones sent the letter for my Des Moines-based attorney to mail. The story was too complicated; I was too weary of it; and Ms. George probably wouldn't have believed me anyway.

Some editors who were persuaded by the facts and felt obliged to acknowledge their unwitting complicity in plagiarism still had reservations. Such was the case with Nancy Dillard at *Poem,* who consulted an attorney and then produced the following statement, inserted into Volume #67 of her periodical as a loose erratum slip:

Poem printed an apparently plagiarized poem in the November 1991 issue under the supposed authorship of David Sumner. The poem, printed as "Someone Forgotten" was in fact the work of Neal Bowers, who first published it in *Poetry* in September 1990, with the title "Tenth-Year

Elegy." *Poem* is happy to acknowledge, with profound apologies to him, the true author of the poem.

Legalistic in tone, the statement seems intended primarily to keep the periodical free of legal entanglements. How a poem can be "apparently plagiarized" and "in fact" someone else's work simultaneously is hard to explain—rather like being uncertainly sure.

Some editors were more definite. Eva Touster and her colleagues at *Cumberland Poetry Review* wrote a direct statement denouncing Jones, as did Bill Trowbridge at the *Laurel Review*, Roger Sheffer at *Mankato Poetry Review*, Kimberly Willardson at *Vincent Brothers Review*, and a few others, probably a half-dozen in all. Outstanding among them for his vigor and clarity was John Keenan, who concluded his commentary in *Four Quarters* by saying,

> Maybe a Clean, Well-Lighted Place is our only refuge. So I am going to clean house and shed light upon the darker side of one person's nature by publicly stating in print: "David S. Jones steals poems written and published by others and submits these poems as his own. He uses the pseudonym **David Sumner.**"

In my experience his forthrightness was the exception rather than the rule.

In addition to confusion about what constitutes plagiarism, most writers are haunted by the fear they may inadvertently appropriate someone else's work. This makes them reluctant to point the finger at anyone else, even when the case is clear-cut. I have personally felt this uneasiness when discovering passages in my work and,

on occasion, entire poems that echo another writer. My
most recent shiver of alarm came after reading Mary
Oliver's "Tasting the Wild Grapes," which captures the
excitement of flushing a fox from the undergrowth and
ends with the following lines:

> . . . you will leap to name it
> as though for the first time, your lit blood
> rushing not to a word but a sound
> small-boned, thin-faced, in a hurry,
> lively as the dark thorns of the wild grapes
> on the unsuspecting tongue!
> The fox! The fox!

What set my heart racing was the realization I, too, had
written a poem about a fox, one I frightened from her
cover of yellow clover while jogging in a field near home.
So struck was I by the encounter that I roughed out a
fairly complete draft of the poem as soon as I returned
from my run, sogging the page with my sweaty hand and
wrist. My poem ends this way:

> Already, she is just a story
> for me to tell, lost in the telling,
> though my friends' faces brighten each time
> with something like joy, and they say,
> "A fox," their voices touched with disbelief,
> needing to name her as I did
> in that sun stunned field, language
> a snare we set to hold at least
> a trace of everything that evades us,
> though it sometimes clamps down tight on
>   air
> and emptiness. "A fox," I say. "A fox."

Because my poem, "The Following Word," was written in 1993 and Mary Oliver's was published in her 1978 *American Primitive,* there's no chance she was influenced by me. And since I'm reasonably sure I had not read her poem until at least a year after writing mine, I can say with as much certainty as I can muster that I was not influenced by hers. Grounded in a literal, personal experience, my poem attempts to capture one of those shining moments of revelation that come all too seldom. I remember everything about its composition and know I did not have a conscious thought about Mary Oliver or her work while drafting the poem. This claim is difficult to substantiate outside my own recollection, however, and if some literary detective should allege I cribbed most of my poem from Oliver, how could I possibly defend myself? Freshman composition students have been skewered with flimsier evidence.

Blame such coincidences on the zeitgeist, the limited number of available subjects and themes, or pure chance. They are still unsettling. The problem is originality and the difficulty of saying anything new. To a great extent, all of us who write are simply repeating those who have written before us and, occasionally, duplicating one another. We hope for distinctive stylistic differences, of course, for a voice that sounds like no one else's; but a quick check of any selection of periodicals will show how rarely that hope is fulfilled. We used to joke in graduate school that the only themes in all of literature are the possibility of love and the inevitability of death. Nothing was said of foxes, although Oliver's and mine flash through a world of transience and lovely mystery that language attempts to capture. Mortality, again.

The trouble with David Jones is not that he sounds like

other poets or shares common subjects and themes with them but that he steals their work. Intent characterizes his appropriations, as does the chronic nature of his activities. These primary markers of the classic plagiarist set him apart from the honest writer, who should have no difficulty making the distinction but in whom Jones evokes feelings of vulnerability. Call it the "first stone syndrome." Few are willing to cast it because they aren't entirely sure of their own originality. Scholars, even more than poets and fiction writers, balk at holding plagiarists accountable, probably because of the cumulative nature of scholarly work. One person's research builds upon everyone else's, and footnotes don't always itemize the total debt. Virtually every scholar believes himself to have been plagiarized and, conversely, worries that his neighbors will find their work unattested in his.

Brilliant or crazy or a little of both, Jones was as devious as he was diligent. Not once did he make a statement that could be used against him as an admission of guilt, and he parried every thrust McKee made. Qualification, explanation, and omission were his techniques. Even when he conceded he had published my work as his own, he stressed that we had "proved" to him he was not the true author he had believed himself to be. Responding in this way, he subtly shifted the blame onto my poems, paradoxically crediting them with the unusual power to imprint his mind.

Such positionings seemed clever to McKee and to us, and we all concluded Jones must have had experience with the law, probably as a defendant in some prior case. His final act of writing to tell me he had returned all contributor's copies of periodicals in which he had published my poems was a way of protecting himself against charges of profiting from his appropriation of my work. This particular defensive action resulted either from legal counseling or from Jones's own shrewd sense of what he needed to do to stay one step ahead of us.

Wishing Jones to be an estimable adversary rather than a fool, I probably gave him more than his due, and so did Nancy. Picking up the photocopied page from *Poet's Market*, the one Jones had included in his box of materials to illustrate his record-keeping methods, she found herself reading it for hidden messages. Marked on the page was the entry for *Howling Dog*, for which the editor offered the following passage as an example of the kind of poetry he typically published:

> you dropped
> your virtue on my foot
> it didn't hurt, but it was hell
>
> trying to get the stain
> off my new sneakers

This seemed to be a periodical to which Jones had submitted poems, according to the marginal notation of a mailing date. But why had he selected this single page and this one periodical to show us? The five lines of doggerel struck Nancy as a taunt. Even the name of the periodical, *Howling Dog*, seemed a calculated slur.

Once Nancy laid out this interpretation for me, it was inescapable. Both of us are inclined, however, to read not simply between the lines but also between the letters in the *words*, handicapped as we are by doctoral degrees in English and by years of literary interpretation. So it was more than possible that we were inventing rather than

receiving Jones's meaning. Given the slightest stimula-
tion, we can find symbolism and nuance in a notice for a
garage sale. And yet Jones was matching us move for
move; we weren't imagining that.

Before parting company with Bruce McKee, we had
him send one last letter to Jones urging him to sign the
simple statement acknowledging his theft of my poems.
Copies were sent by registered and regular mail to Jones's
Oregon address and to his brother's home in Illinois. The
one sent to Aloha was forwarded to an address in Germany. Jones's record of pretended foreign residence made
us doubtful. Even so, all the copies were delivered, and at
least one of them must have reached him, though he never
responded. Apparently, he had nothing more to say; and
when our phone would sometimes ring, with no one
responding when we answered, we became accustomed
to saying, "Hello, Mr. Jones, how are you this evening."
The line would invariably go dead.

Failing to get a further word out of Jones, Nancy
decided she would try to communicate with his wife,
Cynthia. When we learned through Anne Bunch that Cynthia had taken a sudden leave of absence from her teaching job in the Portland area and signed on to teach at a
U.S. military school in Germany, we were led to think she
might be in league with her husband, but we held out
for the possibility that she was ignorant of her husband's
activities.

Writing as someone with her best interest at heart,
Nancy explained the situation to Cynthia and ended with
the following paragraph:

Everyone who hears about this case wonders if you knew
what was going on. I always gave you the benefit of the

doubt. I sensed that this is not the first time things have gotten out of control. I felt that maybe your life has been rearranged in profound ways by other unfortunate actions by David. . . . It would be good if you could respond personally to me so that I will know that David has not intercepted this letter and continued to cover up his actions.

Neither of us knew at the time how accurate Nancy's supposition would prove, but like her husband, Cynthia chose silence. A similar silence emanated from Jones's brother in Illinois, to whom Nancy also sent a copy of her letter.

Family members on both sides of the marriage probably knew nothing of Jones's activities as a plagiarist, but Anne Bunch traced Diane Compton's return address to Cynthia's sister and brother-in-law in the Portland suburb of Milwaukie. Their address, slightly modified, was the one Jones had used with Bruce McKee during their first conversation, and he used it as well for return envelopes of poetry submissions credited to Diane Compton, giving himself not just a separate street and number but also a separate town for his female persona.

When we mentioned to our own friends and associates that we had tried to communicate with Jones's wife and relatives, many of them were distressed. Bad enough for us to obsess about Jones, they felt; it was inappropriate for us to invade the private lives of those around him. "Think of his wife and daughter," they said. Of course, we did think of them. And I didn't like being the disruptive agent in their lives. Unsettling an entire family had not been my intent, and I felt responsible, no matter how much I insisted that Jones had created this situation.

Officials at Glencoe High School acknowledged that

Cynthia had taken an unpaid leave for the 1992–1993 school year but said she left no forwarding address. Administrators at the elementary school their daughter Chloe attended were similarly unable to provide a specific destination, although a clerk there said she recalled a request to transfer Chloe's records to an APO address in New York, probably for a military school in Germany. Anne Bunch, who did her best to locate the Joneses as her final task for Bruce McKee, said it appeared they "do not wish to be found."

For a brief time Nancy and I tried to convince ourselves that pursuing Jones would only push him farther along some obscure escape route. But just when we were about to turn luminous with generosity, other plagiarisms of my poems came to light. There seemed no end to them, especially now that friends and total strangers across the country were looking for anything with the name David Sumner attached to it.

With each new instance, I cared less about the Joneses' dilemma. The only thing I required was an admission of David Jones's guilt, the one thing he seemed determined never to give me. We were perfectly stalemated. If all I could reasonably hope to obtain was more information about him, then Anne Bunch was the person who could supply it, if she would work for us independent of Bruce McKee.

When Nancy phoned, she found Anne eager to continue working on the case. She, like Nancy, sensed there was more to Jones than we had learned thus far. What's more, she and Nancy had developed a friendship over the long-distance lines, and no one could hope for a better ally. As Anne tracked Jones through the Portland area, she was willing to knock on any door, phone any number, and ask any official or clerk or private citizen any question. She talked with Jones's landlady, his neighbors, his postman, his former teachers at Pacific University, editors of local magazines that had published work submitted by him, and followed up any leads they offered. She also requested official information from public records and attempted to find out if he had ever been in trouble with the law in Portland. Hearing from several members of the local arts community that Jones had given a taped reading at a local bookstore, she spent several days trying to find a copy of the recording, without success. She was curious, as we were, to know whose work he had read.

The character portrait she drew from the information she gathered was distinctive. Those who had interacted with Jones described him as "charming," but most of his neighbors said he and his family were aloof. The postal carrier sensed a furtiveness in the way Jones watched from behind the drapes as he delivered the mail and grew exasperated with all the change of address cards, each with a different name, left by Jones when he departed from Aloha. Certain members of the English Department at Pacific University who remembered Jones were quick to stress that he received a master of arts in teaching and not an M.A. in English, although he took courses in their department. They had heard of his plagiarisms and some confided to Anne that they were embarrassed by any association of Jones with their program.

One retired professor had a very particular memory of Jones because Jones had protested his final grade. He characterized him as "engaging in conversation" and "fairly charming" but also capable of demonstrating arrogance and a "general attitude" of anger and unhappiness. He recalled specifically that Jones had confided to him his dissatisfaction with his marriage, complaining so bitterly, in fact, that he left the impression a divorce was imminent. He also remembered that Jones once told him he "had been teaching and wasn't too happy with that." At one point, Jones had shown him some of his poems in the hope that an independent study course in poetry writing could be arranged. The professor declined because "There was something in his attitude." Also, he said, "I didn't care for the poems he was showing me."

Secretive, brooding, chronically unemployed, and miserable in his life, Jones appears to exhibit some of the primary markers of the antisocial personality. Recognizing this, Anne Bunch, unflappable in every other way, became a little more cautious in her pursuit, telling Nancy she thought Jones was "strange." Still she and Nancy kept searching for the clue to Jones's true identity. Their primary point of investigation was his alleged membership in the teaching profession. Why, they asked one another, had a man with a master's degree in teaching been unemployed for more than four years? Apart from bad luck or plain laziness, the only possible explanation was some kind of trouble. An inquiry filed with the Oregon Teacher Standards and Practices Commission might turn up the answer.

6.

Behind the Masks

THE REPORT on Jones's status as a teacher was a small opening, one Anne Bunch recognized immediately, causing her to phone excitedly with the news when it reached her office. The specifics of the report revealed that Jones had taught in the Centralia, Illinois, School District and in Roseburg, Oregon, School District 4, and included the following:

> Applicant held Oregon Basic Teaching License with basic elementary and handicapped endorsements from 3/80 through 3/83 and a Basic Teaching License with basic elementary endorsement from 3/83 through 3/86. The Commission revoked applicant's Oregon teaching license effective 3/26/86.

According to Oregon law, "public access to general information in files maintained by public agencies" is allowed "while reserving the right to withhold certain information potentially injurious to the affected party." In other words, we could know that Jones had been kicked out of the teaching profession but could not be told why. Shielded by the same agency that had expelled him, Jones remained hidden; but we now had some clues. And we understood why he had found work so hard to obtain in his "area," as he had written to Bruce McKee.

Following the lead closest to hand, Anne phoned the Roseburg School District office and asked the secretary if she knew David Jones. Although the secretary said Jones had been a second grade teacher in two Roseburg schools "approximately seven or eight years ago," she clearly had cause to remember him. His departure had been "a very sensitive area," she said. Gradually, more information was forthcoming as Anne tactfully asked if Jones had left "under stressful conditions." Making certain Anne understood that she was revealing nothing that was not on the public record, the secretary directed her to the local newspaper, the *Roseburg News-Review.* There Anne could find stories of Jones's trial and conviction for sexually molesting several of his second grade female students at Green Elementary School.

This information settled on our lives in Ames, Iowa, like toxic debris from a chemical explosion. First the boom of revelation; then the poisonous after-effects. Initially stunned, neither of us wanted to believe it and found ourselves curiously on David Jones's side. The name was so common, almost generic, a mistake could easily be made. But Anne Bunch was much too exacting to go that far wrong. The newspaper clippings she sent, and the official record of his incarceration in the Oregon State Penitentiary, left no room for doubt. Our David Jones, alias David Sumner et al., was a child molester.

I felt so tainted even by my remote and involuntary association with Jones I wanted to keep this news to myself and told Nancy we should drop our pursuit of him immediately. When we last had him in view, he was an unrepentant copyist, but he had turned a corner and undergone a loathsome transformation. The fact that he claimed to have found me through my poems, actually to have chosen me because of some affinity he felt with me and my work, brought back my original feelings of violation and intensified them.

Jones was indicted by a grand jury on six counts of sexual abuse and faced his victims one at a time in three separate trials between June 11, 1985 and February 7, 1986. Newspaper accounts of the courtroom procedures are painful to read, primarily because Oregon law at the time permitted the defendant's attorney to question the victims on the witness stand. The first trial ended in acquittal, after the jury had deliberated for less than an hour; and the second trial ended in identical fashion. In both instances, the girls accusing Jones of sexually molesting them were discredited by Jones's attorney because they had not reported the incidents immediately. Jones took the stand himself in each case and denied all charges. Describing his classroom as being as busy as a bus station, even during recess when the incidents allegedly occurred, he insisted it would be impossible to do the things he was accused of without being caught. Further, he said he had no idea why any of his students would make such charges against him.

The young girls in both of these trials exhibited the classic characteristics of sexual abuse. Each was described by her parents as having undergone behavioral changes, including sleep disruption and mood swings. Each had delayed telling her parents because of embarrassment and fear that Mr. Jones would punish her in some way. Despite these revealing markers, however, both juries believed Jones. The deputy district attorney who tried both cases spoke with Nancy at length about his recollection of the trials and expressed lingering bitterness over the way the little girls had been humiliated by Jones's attorney, who ridiculed their charges and confused them with questions about the dates and locations of the molestations. When told of Jones's current activities as a plagiarist, he said he understood "the workings of the criminal mind" well enough not to be surprised.

The third trial, like the first two, included a jury trip to the elementary school and the classroom where Jones had taught. As in the previous trials, Jones's lawyer did his best to confuse the girl and this time went so far as to suggest that she had invented the story after talking to a social worker who visited the school and planted the idea in her mind. Once more, Jones took the stand and empha-sized the openness and accessibility of his classroom to any passersby. Directly contradicting the girl's testimony, he claimed she had never been seated at the back of the room, where she claimed the molestations occurred, but had been placed by him at the front because she had been eating crayons and pencils and drinking glue. This time, however, Jones's charm failed him. After more than ten hours of deliberation, the jury returned a guilty verdict on two counts of first degree sexual abuse.

On the day of his sentencing, David Jones said in his own behalf he posed no risk to the community in which he was living, presumably hoping to persuade the judge not to imprison him. Responding that he had taken into account the abuse, the age of the victim, and the "special situation" of a teacher found guilty of abusing the public trust, the judge then sentenced Jones to two concurrent five-year terms. By imposing no minimum time, he noted that he was leaving open the possibility of parole in six to ten months. Indicating his intention to appeal, Jones's attorney was able to get him released on bail, a mere $500 because, as the judge acknowledged, he had always appeared in court as scheduled.

Using the possibility of an appeal as a negotiating tool, Jones and his attorney bargained with the district attorney to have two additional charges of sexual abuse dismissed in return for Jones's willingness to serve the prison term already imposed upon him. In striking this agreement, Jones dropped his threat of appeal, avoided a fourth trial, and obtained a binding promise that the young girl bringing the charges against him could not file them at some point in the future. On February 11, 1986, Jones entered the state penitentiary at Salem, was transferred to the Santiam Correction Institution on May 2 and was paroled on July 27, 1986. Even his parole officer confided to Anne Bunch that six months in prison and six months on parole constituted a very slight punishment for the crime of sexually abusing seven-year-old girls.

During his trials, Jones employed the strategies he subsequently used when confronted about his plagiarism, denying culpability and offering a glib alternative version of the facts. As I read the accounts of his testimony, I could hear his voice on McKee's tape recordings, unemotional, almost ingenuous. "Noooo," he had said when McKee asked him if he knew anything about stolen poems. He must have sounded like that when confronted with the abuse of children. There was in him a chilling calmness, with just a touch of breathlessness, as if he were exhilarated by the nearness of his accusers.

We now knew things about Jones that we would have

preferred not to know. The impenitent plagiarist seemed benign alongside the treacherous teacher. But, of course, we couldn't unknow what we had learned, having followed Jones one turn too far to find our way back to an earlier ignorance. As far as I was concerned, our pursuit was over; but Nancy was less ready to leave the chase. She was determined to make a final move. In a three-page letter mailed to Jones at his wife's and brother's addresses, she began by warning that should he decide to return to the Portland area he would find that people there "now know about your illegal activities, your real name, your wife's name, your thefts, your lies, and your various aliases." She then presented a bulleted listing of the individuals and groups with whom we had been in touch and concluded with a long paragraph of biographical data beginning with the following statement: "In case you think I am bluffing about what I know, let me tell you . . . " followed by details ranging from his social security number to his height and weight, his mother's maiden name, and the name of the bank that financed his car. Then, in a final act of bravado, she added before closing, "Was it really worth it? Try it again and see what happens."

I had nothing at all to say to Jones, nor did I imagine he had anything to communicate to me, except perhaps more lies and evasions. Nancy and I both worried about his daughter, Chloe. Hard enough for us to understand why Cynthia had stuck by her husband through his child abuse trials and brief stay in prison, we couldn't imagine why she permitted him in the same home as their daughter. Nancy was so concerned about this that she put the question to Cynthia in a letter telling her we knew of David's criminal past. There was no response.

In a final attempt to locate Jones, Nancy contacted the federal agency that, according to Anne Bunch's research, had investigated Cynthia Jones before employing her to teach at Rose Barracks in Sorghof, Germany. Stating that Cynthia had possibly taken the job to assist her husband in his flight from the United States and a potential lawsuit prompted a quick reply from Elizabeth Suratt, an investigator with the U.S. Army–Europe. Speaking with Nancy by phone, Suratt confirmed that Cynthia was in residence there but insisted David was not. Whether he was living somewhere else in Germany or had returned to the U.S. was information she was unwilling or unable to provide. Nancy then forwarded to Ms. Suratt not only evidence of Jones's plagiarisms but also the clippings concerning his trials and conviction in Roseburg, Oregon. She received no further communication from Ms. Suratt.

In the end, all efforts to locate Jones failed, though we suspected he might be staying with his brother in Illinois or with his wife's sister and her husband in Milwaukie, Oregon. Tempting as it was to set Anne Bunch on the trail once more, or to travel ourselves to find and confront him, we chose to let him disappear, although we were troubled by his physical anonymity. Except for the general description of his height and weight, we didn't know what he looked like and could imagine that he was any tall stranger.

To end this uncertainty, Nancy obtained, through her contact with the Douglas County, Oregon, district attorney's office, a copy of Jones's mug shots—two photos, one showing a glum David Jones with glasses and curly hair, the other showing the same face without glasses and hair. Although there was nothing particularly funny about the photographs, Nancy and I both began laughing when they arrived, partly because of the rush we felt at having this visual information, but mostly because the two poses revealed so perfectly the doubleness of the man. "Mr. Sumner and Mr. Jones," I said, "but which is which?" "Definitely, the toupee goes with Sumner," Nancy shot back. We conjured up a ceremony in which David Jones would don spectacles and wig to become David Sumner, plagiarist. And so there he was at last, duplicity personified.

Long before we knew Jones's criminal history, we had enlisted the aid of a friend who is a practicing psychologist in Ames. We asked her to review the information we had collected on David Jones and to offer her best long-distance professional opinion about his motivations. In her view Jones is a sociopath whose compulsive plagiarism is rooted in feelings of inadequacy and a desire to become someone else. She felt reasonably certain we would discover he had been in trouble before and urged us to trace his work record and search for any criminal history. I recall thinking that she had carried her psycho-analytic skills too far, just as Nancy and I sometimes go too far in our interpretation of symbols and nuances of meaning. But she had seen in the facts about Jones and heard in his voice on the tape a type of person familiar to her in her practice. Others in the counseling field would come forward later to confirm her diagnosis.

Apart from wanting to know who was stealing my poems, the most frequently asked question was *Why?* We asked it many times ourselves, assuming there had to be a logical explanation. The best we could do was to hypothesize that Jones was trying to invent a new identity for himself so he could return to teaching. If he could literally become David Sumner, whose bibliography grew extensively in only two years, he could possibly find employment at a community college or maybe even as a writer in the schools. This was a good theory, but it didn't account for Jones's other pseudonyms—Diane Compton, in particular. He couldn't literally become her without a very elaborate transformation, indeed.

The problem, of course, was trying to understand Jones's behavior as if it proceeded from rational motivations. Asking why he would steal poems and publish them under various pseudonyms is no easier question than asking why he sexually molested the little girls in his second grade classroom. Elizabeth Biller, a poet and psychotherapist in Palo Alto, California, described the dilemma to me this way:

> The problem for people like yourself, and myself, and most of mankind in encountering the likes of Sumner/Jones is in absorbing the dawning realization, not of injury—while awful, people injure themselves & each other all the time—but, that this "human being" does not operate as we do, emotionally and morally. I am speaking of what has been rather loosely called the psychopathic personality for whom psychotherapy & other means of persuasion to change do not work, because the usual leverages can acquire no purchase: there is no there, there: no true empathy, no true remorse. But there is, sometimes, a cunning, even a charm, which can discern what it is that someone wants to hear; when that is then said (as in the expressions of gratitude/ contrition by S-J), it is, however, for a strategic reason: for the perpetrator's own perceived advantage.

The risks of psychoanalyzing someone not physically present are obvious, but Biller recognized Jones from her experience and training, just as our psychologist friend in Ames knew him from the details of his activities. Also, as I've said, Nancy and others from the beginning sensed in Jones something off-center and threatening. Supporting such intuitive assessments Biller says:

> When I was in training I was told, "You know when you're in the room with a psychopath when the hairs on the back of your neck stand up." Some diagnostic sign!! But accurate, as a cue for "counter-transference."

Looking now at Jones's behavior and even at the poems he chose to represent as his own, I wonder how I could not have suspected he was driven by something more than literary larceny. Many of Jones's published poems, including nearly all of those we know to have been plagiarized, are about parents or parent-child relationships. My "Tenth-Year Elegy" fits this pattern, as does "RSVP," with its implicit death in the family. And the other two poems Jones lifted from the September 1990 *Poetry* are specifically about fathers, as is the poem by Sharon Olds he stole, "My Father Snoring." Collectively these poems represent the father as negligent, noncommunicative, diseased and dying, domineering, or simply absent. Although sometimes tinged with sadness and regret, their undercurrent of anger, resentment, or despair may have attracted Jones.

When poets ponder the concept of audience, they tend to think of the reader encountering the poem in a pristine setting where both are earnest and, in some fundamental way, innocent. I have often glibly maintained that my concept of audience is the single reader who might pick up my poem, if I dropped it on the street, and find it speaks to him. I never thought the person stooping to retrieve my page might be someone like David Jones, a creature with needs and urges that make absolutely no sense to me and with whom I desire no communication. Thinking of him discovering "Tenth-Year Elegy" in *Poetry* and finding that it throbbed in his own wound brings me closer to him than I wish to be.

Some of my theory-minded colleagues have chided me for feeling this way, pointing out that I gave up control of my poems as soon as I allowed them to be published. A few have gone further, arguing that my insistence on ownership is a denial of the communal nature of art. They say each reader creates his own text in the act of reading. So Jones is just one more person laying claim to the text. That he sometimes republishes what he reads is perhaps only an extension of the process. If his reception of the poem is unique, as they reason, then the intent that drives him to offer it as his own must be similarly original, and what he publishes is just as much his as what he reads.

While I doubt that Jones thought in these terms when he was copying down my work, I do believe he benefited from the contemporary intellectual climate. (I think particularly of recent poetry collections, one in which the poet leaves out words for the reader to supply and another which is a collage of other people's lines.) In fact, had he underpinned his activities with theory, he might have found vigorous defenders among literary theorists. At the very least, one of them would surely have written a paper characterizing Jones as the epitome of the postmodern reader/poet. One may do it yet.

Initially the revelations of Jones's deviant past very nearly persuaded me not to tell this story at all. Among the liabilities, as I saw them, were the chance that I would be perceived as disclosing damaging information to get back at Jones, and the possibility that his criminal record would make his activities as a plagiarist seem inconsequential. But learning of his past was part of my experience as his victim, and his actions in regard to me made a different kind of sense once I knew the worst about him. Insofar as Jones's behavior can be understood, pedophilia and plagiarism seem to be expressions of his need to control, especially in a secretive way.

An additional liability of revealing Jones's criminal past is implying that all plagiarists are pathological. Unmask a plagiarist and find a child molester is not the message I want to send, knowing that plagiarists are often driven by much more pragmatic urges—the pressure to publish to gain tenure, for example. At the same time, I can't help feeling that the concept of the respectable plagiarist is at least oxymoronic. That we harbor such a notion at all indicates how uncertain we are about those who steal the words and ideas of others. Ironically, Jones's personal history may be his best defense against charges of plagiarism, simply because it deflects attention and gives those already squeamish about the subject of literary ownership an easy way out. "Jones is not your typical plagiarist," they say. Indeed, but then who is?

7.

What's News?

WITHIN A year after the discovery of Jones's first plagiarism of my work, word of his activities had spread so
extensively that I regularly heard from interested strangers. Some wanted to commiserate, others to share their
own experiences and views. Now and then, someone sent
a poem that seemed suspect or told me of a plagiarism I
had already found. As heartening as this voluntary assistance was, I began to worry that the David Jones story
was mutating, the way oral narratives invariably do. I
remembered the old party game, Gossip, in which messages are whispered ear to ear around a large circle of people until what began as "A ship foundered on the rocks of
chance" becomes "Slip me a quarter and hold onto your
pants." Such alterations can happen, as I knew from an
embellished account of Gregory Orr's own troubles with
plagiarism. The story told to me featured personal confrontation between Orr and his thief when, in fact, things
were settled easily enough by Orr's publisher.

Some correspondents saw fictional possibilities in my
experience. Many urged me to write a novel, one writer

going so far as to donate a plot outline with a villain named Sumner at the center of what he envisioned as a "Holmesian" tale. Accurate or inaccurate, the story was abroad, and I was associated one way or another with plagiarism. For a while I considered making public statements through letters-to-the-editor columns in various periodicals; but no letter could do justice to the story's complexities. Something more substantial was needed, so when Peter Blocksom, the managing editor of *Writer's Digest*, invited me to write a piece for *Writer's Yearbook 1994*, I gladly produced a factual outline of the case complete with recommendations for handling future plagiarism cases. Despite my assertion that peer review of complaints coupled with public exposure of the plagiarist in well-respected periodicals would help, I knew such a system wouldn't have stopped Jones. The weaknesses he revealed in the body poetic were too widespread to be healed by nostrums, if at all. And I came to understand that the important challenge was not finding a way to stop a future David Jones but evaluating the medium in which the current one had prospered.

With this larger view in mind, I wrote another essay, "A Loss for Words: Plagiarism and Silence," which Joseph Epstein was kind enough to publish in *The American Scholar*. Raising more questions than I could answer, I argued a metaphor of contagion, comparing Jones to an invasive virus and defining plagiarism as a loss of language that begins with the original infection and becomes a greater silence characterized by neglect and inaction in the literary and academic world. Surely the cure for silence is language, I reasoned, and did my best to shatter the mute air with my own voice. In this was a kind of catharsis, a final coming to terms with the bizarre person who misused my work and me, and it felt good to say to those who doubted the significance of his actions that they were wrong.

While the essay was awaiting publication, I put David Jones out of mind, and Nancy and I agreed we had brought the matter to as good a close as could be hoped for. Mindful of how little response was generated by the *Writer's Digest* article and conditioned by several years of general silence, I thought the essay might provoke a comment from one or two academics or workshop writers taking umbrage at my negative characterization of the current state of poetry. There was also the chance some readers would recognize Jones's modus operandi and introduce me to new instances of his thefts. Despite such unhappy expectations, I looked forward to publication of what I thought would be my final words on the case and the chance to bid David Jones farewell. I hadn't counted on the journalists, however.

Within a few weeks of the essay's appearance in *The American Scholar's* Fall 1994 issue, I was besieged by phone calls from newspaper reporters who had read it. *The New York Times, The Chronicle of Higher Education, The Cleveland Plain Dealer,* and *The Des Moines Register* requested interviews and additional information. To each I sent Nancy's documentation, 60 single-spaced pages chronicling events from the moment we learned that David Jones had entered our lives to the moment we received the very request we were answering. Supplying the complete file was overkill, perhaps, but such abundant evidence smoothed the skeptical brow and made the eye widen in amazement rather than doubt. As it turned out, I need not have worried about the journalists' attitudes. For them, plagiarism was not an occasion for philosophical maundering but for indignation and action.

Because their world is a pragmatic one built on facts, journalists see plagiarism for what it is—the theft of someone else's creative and intellectual property. Journalists who plagiarize are ruined. They lose their jobs and reputations, unlike academicians, who rarely suffer severe consequences for taking someone else's work. I sensed immediately in each reporter an empathy manifested much less uniformly among writers, editors, and my university colleagues. Apart from whatever they saw as newsworthy in the story, they seemed intent on exposing Jones. Finally I had found allies willing to call a thief a crook rather than a confused or misguided soul plagued by insecurities or a photographic memory. Their enthusiasm amazed and invigorated me, although it also rushed me back into the mental room where Jones was locked away. Sometimes, when a reporter called to ask a question or clarify a detail, I was overwhelmed by claustrophobia, a breathless fear I had shut the door from the wrong side and couldn't get out.

Here, at last, was vindication. Here, too, was further association with plagiarism, hardly what I would have chosen as my entrée into the public's awareness. During twenty-five years of publishing poems in periodicals and books, I had never received a fraction of the attention two stolen poems had generated; and I couldn't escape feeling this was another manifestation of how thoroughly Jones had contaminated my life and work—to be better known for what was taken from me than for what I had given.

My ambivalence intensified when William Grimes's fine account in *The New York Times* was reprinted in newspapers throughout the country and around the world (notably, in *The International Herald Tribune*), stimulated further stories in *The London Times* and *The Australian*, and prompted an interview on the Canadian Broadcasting Corporation radio program "As It Happens." Suddenly the silence I bemoaned in *The American Scholar* essay became a great noise, which left me grateful but also troubled. If anecdotal accounts of plagiarism could follow my fellow poets and victims Gregory Orr and Henry Taylor for decades, carried merely by the breath, how could I hope ever to escape the talk after this gale of publicity: "Bowers, yes, wasn't he involved in some plagiarism mess a few years ago?"

Of more immediate concern was my mail, which quadrupled in volume and contained extraordinary letters. Not only was I now a clearinghouse for others who believed themselves plagiarized or otherwise wronged, I was also a contact who could be tapped for favors. The requests ranged from the straightforward business proposition— an opportunity to buy computer software guaranteed to "snare" 80 percent of student plagiarists—to an invitation to meet with a poet from India to critique his poems while he visited the United States with his wife, who had won the trip in a sporting quiz contest. There was an offer to join an anticircumcision organization, because as a victim of plagiarism I would no doubt share its views, one loss being much like another, I suppose. One correspondent simply wanted to inform me an article about me had appeared in *The New York Times* and to offer a copy of it, in case I hadn't seen it. A similar, though truncated, message turned up on my office answering machine, an elderly female voice saying, "I read about your plagiarism case." No further remarks, no name, and no phone number.

The president of a consortium asked me to serve as agent for a young Englishwoman who wrote poems. Left in a coma by a horrible automobile accident, she returned to consciousness accompanied by the muse (who must also have been injured in the crash, judging by the work she inspired). This gentleman enclosed materials concerning his extensive plans to produce 3-D photographs of the treasures of the Vatican, the Louvre, and the Prado. A previous project of his had been a manuscript on "multiple murder and demonic possession." But for the moment he was intent on my helping find a publisher for his protégé's work.

Among the many scientists who wrote to tell me plagiarism and the theft of research is much worse in their field than in poetry, one contended that an effective cancer treatment is being kept from development by a man who "wormed his way into the National Academy of Sciences by plagiarism" and is exercising control over various laboratory projects. Another writer attacked the Clinton health care plan, claiming it failed because it was plagiarized and those who stole it didn't know how to make it work. And a mathematician sent a packet of documents to support his contention that he was robbed of his discovery of several nineteenth-century letters mentioning an ancient precursor to the computer. He asserted, "It seems like the entire legal superstructure of the country has collapsed under my plagiarism complaint. The wall of silence of the media-academic complex has been incredible."

To illustrate his frustration in the search for justice, the mathematician enclosed letters he wrote to President and Mrs. Clinton, Attorney General Janet Reno, and the Secret Service, all complaining bitterly about his loss of intellectual property and seeking restitution. Other documents proposed the disbarment of certain attorneys he believed had wronged him and the rescission of degrees earned by his perceived enemies. In one letter, he mused, "It makes no sense to me why Clinton is passing up an opportunity to look good by speaking out against plagiarism." Most notable, perhaps, was the following paragraph:

> Also in early October, 1994, Nobel Prizes will be announced, and I will find out if I have been nominated for giving no peace to the scientific/research/education establishment on my plagiarism complaint. This news would be a wild card that could drastically change the outcome of the November, 1994 elections. "A vote for me is a vote to impeach Bill Clinton" might become a popular campaign theme.

Hearing this man's aggrieved and excessive voice, I think of my own ardent claims of injury, and wonder how near the edge I have come, my feet in the sliding shale. I haven't written letters to the White House or imagined myself the victim in some conspiracy of silence perpetrated by the "media-academic complex," but what if the casual observer notes only a qualitative difference between me and my ranting correspondent? Could I be mistaken for someone who has slept in the ditch of compulsion, day after day plodding the road, leafleting the towns? Disavow it though I might, I also advance a candidacy: A vote for me is a vote for the integrity of poetry and for honesty and justice and goodness and maybe down comforters on a chilly night. Where does it end, this advocacy?

Poets grow accustomed to encounters with intense and sometimes wild-eyed people. Usually they want to talk about their work or about creativity and inspiration. They often appear at my office door, sent by a colleague relieved to point in my direction while slipping away.

Stirred by an urge to create or simply to be a creative person, these occasional visitors are part of my life as a poetry teacher in a large land-grant university, and I do my utmost to respect and reinforce their best impulses. Now that the queue has been lengthened to include delusional paranoids, however, I worry that my door has been marked with a kind of hobo sign meaning kindred spirit.

As if to feed such insecurities, the author of a monograph on plagiarism wrote, "It's debatable in this strange realm whether the hunter or the hunted is the odder," and then argued that wrongful accusations of intellectual and literary theft are commonplace. And another "expert" on the subject asked abrasively what sort of punishment I would prefer for my thief: "Emasculation? Burning at the Stake?" Accusing me of being "a little excessive" in my pursuit of Jones, he advised that although my poems might have been cheapened by plagiarism, they had not actually been taken away from me.

Although I tried not to let the spiteful writers bother me, they were hard to dismiss because they attacked me personally—and for nothing more than having the temerity to speak out against the theft of my work. Like abusive nurses who slap the patient when he moans, they meant to teach me stoicism and silence. It's a rough medicine that blames the body for its injury, but there is a certain expediency in its practice. After the first few backhands, the sufferer is likely to declare himself cured and flee the premises—one more successful treatment. In my own case, these therapists found me odd, intemperate, immodest, and deserving of victimization, not because my poems were good but because I was weak. Of my plagiarist, they offered no opinion, finding him irrelevant to their considerations.

Among those correspondents unhappy with me, the most distressing was the vascular surgeon who complained of the unfortunate coincidence of having David Jones's pseudonym as his real name. He was embarrassed and somewhat angry to see the name David Sumner featured in *The New York Times* so negatively:

> Although the *Times* identifies David Sumner as the plagiarist, not until the second page is his true identity (David Jones) revealed. To make matters worse, this David Jones is from Illinois and attended Southern Illinois University, where I teach. Also, we share the same middle initial, which I hope he hasn't used in his pseudonym.

Worried about his reputation and already tired of jokes by his friends and associates, Dr. Sumner pointed out "one's name is part of one's identity," and expressed his wish that the name had been identified as a pseudonym at the beginning of the various articles and then used "less frequently and less disparagingly."

Until hearing from the good doctor, I assumed that Jones's choice of pseudonym was either random or suggested by his brother's residence in Sumner, Illinois. Now, it seems possible he took it from Dr. Sumner, coming by it when he lived in Carbondale and attended Southern Illinois University. I wonder if inquiries might reveal that a Diane Compton has been similarly mistreated.

That a plagiarist of poetry may have plagiarized his pen name is altogether fitting, although I suspect Dr. Sumner doesn't appreciate the perverse irony such consistency represents. Displeased rather than reflective, he seems intent in his letter to hold me accountable for his discomfort. And why not? But for the noise I made in public places, David Sumner/Jones might have continued his false career unnoticed.

In truth I wish I were not standing in a public place, telling this story. It's difficult enough to maintain an image of stability when everyone expects a poet to be a little odd. Even here in peaceful Ames, Iowa, where the citizens have grown accustomed to eccentricities from some professors at the university (like the scientist who recommended blowing up the moon to improve the weather), I get occasional knowing looks. Small wonder if those unacquainted with me wag their heads, although I routinely wear a coat and tie to confound expectations of how a poet should look. Clean shaven and with a Windsor knot under his chin, a poet is still a poet, which is to say, odd.

To make matters worse, I've experienced additional thefts of my work right here in my hometown. It's as if I've been "chosen," the way some folks claim to have been selected for repeated abductions by aliens. Some of my less charitable colleagues are probably betting I will next claim my poems have been beamed aboard a flying saucer, the first case of intergalactic plagiarism.

Actually, things are much more down to earth. During the height of David Jones's activities, I gave a poetry reading at a local book store and noticed lovely framed calligraphies adorning the walls. Idling over to look at them, I was shocked to discover that their texts were my poems, not the same ones Jones had taken, which would have been too much coincidence to endure. When I inquired of the manager how he came to have these works, which were marked $200 each, he produced from behind the counter a beautiful little handmade book presenting another of my poems in calligraphy. This one had a price tag of $400. On loan from a boutique, the pieces were for sale, he told me, and was stunned that I knew nothing of this commercial venture employing my work.

The calligrapher was someone known to me, so I thought personal communication the best way to deal with the problem. Drafting a letter, I said I had not given permission to use my poems and certainly not to make money from their reproduction in any form. Her reply was simply that, as a calligrapher, she felt entitled to use whatever texts she pleased, since she was transforming them into her own art. In fact, she had been undertaking such transformations for a long time and had presented works by Frost and Thoreau (not bad company for misery), routinely offering pieces for sale. Only the most strenuous protests and the threat of a lawsuit dissuaded her from continuing to use my poems, and even then she remained unconvinced she had done anything wrong.

Her attitude toward other people's poetry was essentially the same as Jones's: it was there for the taking. More directly than Jones, however, my calligrapher-copyist was engaged in commercialization. By moving poems from the printed page to the matted board suitable for hanging above the sofa, she literally regarded them as commodities. The price she attached to them was sufficient to recover the cost of her materials and still leave a modest profit, after paying a percentage to the store owner who was vending them. Had I been asked to share in this enterprise, I'm not sure I would have been interested, preferring to think of poetry as something other than decor.

Viewing this additional larceny against the background of my ongoing struggle with David Jones, many of my acquaintances remarked I was having a run of bad luck. Several made observations about fate, and nearly everyone consoled me with the "you-should-feel-flattered" line. At the same time, I fear they were beginning to classify me with the bleaters and chest-beaters who always have another injustice to bemoan. Virtually every conversation began with a question about my poetry thieves, which was rather like asking Job how his boils are today. "Had any poems stolen lately?" replaced inquiries about how my writing was going.

Worsening this view was an even more public theft of my work: a poem of mine cast in bronze and located on the Iowa State University campus was pried from the metal base to which it was attached. Titled "Art Thief," it commemorated a whimsical aluminum sculpture, "Flat Rabbit," stolen while I was completing a series of commissioned poems featuring campus art. Intended as an indictment of anyone who would steal art, the poem was installed where "Flat Rabbit" once stood, as a literal kind of poetic justice. Because it was the property of the university and, ultimately, the state of Iowa, the bronzed poem's disappearance prompted stories in local papers, each of them emphasizing the irony of an art thief stealing a poem titled "Art Thief" and publicizing a $250 reward for its recovery. Printed alongside the newspaper articles, my poem, an imagined monologue, gave the villain the last word:

ART THIEF

All art defines itself
by what's left out:
the city in Gauguin's paradise,
corners in Henry Moore.

Think of Renoir's vase
filled with chrysanthemums,
how the room has disappeared,
the tabletop itself barely a suggestion.

My technique perfects such absences.
It's what astonishes:
the empty hook, the blank place
on the wall, the vacant pedestal.

I leave behind the plaque
to name the space,
the pure ideal you wanted
all along but didn't realize,

and lumber into darkness
with a load of imperfections
heavy on my back.
No need to thank me.

Written several years before I ever heard of David Sumner/Jones, this poem does his ilk too much credit by implying that a philosophy or aesthetic underpins their deeds. Taking on the same assignment today, I doubt that I would make my apologist for the thieves so contemplative. Such is the difference between considering the theft of someone else's work and enduring the theft of one's own. Of course, Jones never removed my work completely, although some of my neighbors did speculate that he stole the plaque. Until the university cleared away the twisted, empty base that formerly held the plaque, it stood as a symbol of my main preoccupation of the past three years.

There are days when I wonder where the next plagiarism will occur. Whatever befalls me in the coming years here in America's heartland, I can never expect to be thought of simply as a poet. I am now "that poet whose work was stolen," and the embellishments upon that clause will be varied and imaginative. It's difficult for me, as well, to think of myself in the old way. Whenever I sit down to write a poem, my thoughts drift to David Jones, and I wonder if I may be creating more material for him (or someone else) to steal. One wag recently predicted that Jones would probably lift something from this very book. I felt myself flinch at the remark. My only defense against such an intrusion is the book itself, written not to get even but to even out my life, to recover my poetic imperative if not my poetry. Maybe I have made progress in the right direction, but this story has no final refuge.

It seems I have stopped Jones from taking my work, as far as I know, but haven't completely closed his counterfeiting shop. Consequently, this story ends where it began, with a theft and a disguise. Possibly, Jones has entered a new phase and genre, stealing fiction and offering it for publication under the name Paul G. Schmidt. When Schmidt submitted an Ethan Canin story to *The Gettysburg Review*, the plagiarism was quickly exposed, and the editor, Peter Stitt, wrote Schmidt, admonishing him: "I don't know whether you habitually do this sort of thing, but if you do, I urge you to desist immediately. It is an extremely ugly thing to do and can get you in nothing but the most serious of trouble." The response to Stitt was a form letter, with blanks for citing the story's title and real author, and included the following disclaimer:

The submission of this story to your journal was part of a scientific research study of factors influencing acceptance for publication of short fiction by literary journals and mass audience magazines. Five previously published short stories were submitted for consideration, each to twenty different periodicals. This research study is still in process [sic] and results are just beginning to come in.

Therefore, I urgently request your cooperation in maintaining the confidential nature of this investigation for a period of no longer than one year from the date of submission of the story to your periodical.

When the *Sewanee Review*'s editor, George Core, received the same story for consideration, he tried to help lay a trap for Schmidt by expressing interest in the submission. At my request, Core asked Schmidt for a phone number, ostensibly to talk about the story at their mutual convenience. Perhaps sensing an ambush, Schmidt replied with a form letter similar to that sent to Stitt. Had a phone number been provided, Core would have passed it along to me, and I would have phoned Schmidt to test whether or not he is David Jones. Having heard Jones's voice on the tapes made by my attorney, Nancy and I feel we could easily recognize him, even if he denied his identity.

Failing to connect with Mr. Schmidt directly, we made the best of what he had already given us, his handwriting. Nancy took copies of Schmidt's and Jones's script to a certified handwriting expert who regularly testifies in legal cases. Her conclusion: 100 percent certainty that Schmidt and Jones are the same person. But what astonished us was the precise character portrait of Jones she voluntarily offered. Without being told anything about him, she described David Jones, right down to his antisocial compulsions and his time in jail.

Paul G. Schmidt receives mail at a Summerland Key, Florida post office box, but he is unlisted in any of the area phone directories. Our limited efforts to find him exactly paralleled our initial attempts to locate David Sumner, leading us to conclude he can't be found because he exists only as David Jones's invention, a Schmidt (Smith) seemingly calculated to balance Jones.

If Schmidt and Jones are the same person, my plagiarist has moved not only into a new genre but also into a new mode of plagiarism, one with a fail-safe mechanism. Each time he is caught, he can claim a "scientific research study," asserting that the story in question is not stolen but part of an experiment. If the story is accepted by an editor who does not recognize it, Schmidt need only add another item to his false bibliography. Instead of running away from accusations and evidence, he can stay put; and should his phone ring with a lawyer on the other end, he has a ready response. Presumably, even if Schmidt's disguise is stripped away, he can say it is part of the research project, a necessary distancing of himself from the materials.

Although he did not change the title of Canin's story, a departure from Jones's technique of renaming poems, Schmidt did make small changes in the text comparable to the tinkerings in my poems. These alterations betray a compulsive need to claim the work being copied, and belie the assertion of scientific objectivity. In any case, such a research project as Schmidt claims is implausible. No respectable researcher would undertake such a venture without the consent of authors whose works are circulated under another name. And what would an experiment of deception prove except that editors take it on faith that contributors submit their own work for consideration?

Ethan Canin's agent, when informed by Peter Stitt of the plagiarism, responded, "I think that Schmidt is either nuts or working on a story about great writing rejected by editors when sent unsolicited." She did not indicate any plans for further investigation though Stitt urged her to do something, "since this sort of thing is so very, very reprehensible."

Whether or not Paul G. Schmidt is David Jones, he is out there, engaged in a deception of immense proportions. Using the figures he provided in his form letter to Peter Stitt, we can determine that he has submitted stolen short stories to as many as 100 different literary periodicals. He even submitted the Canin story, "Emperor of the Air," to *The Atlantic*, where it was originally published. Whatever he lacks in imagination, he makes up for in audacity; but then he knows by now the risks are small. And he can always transform himself into another identity, dabbling perhaps in another genre. Unless he chooses to stop himself, he will be with us all for a long time, I suspect. Selfish of me, I know, but I'm glad to have him out of poetry and, at least in the immediate sense, out of my life.

Some people have offered the opinion that David Jones is my reverse *doppelganger*, a secret sharer in my poetry who is my exact opposite. Even though I am fond of paradox, it's difficult to conceptualize a person who is identical to me but completely different at the same time. The truth is that Jones and I have some curious points of coincidence: same height, approximately the same weight, both in our forties, both in the teaching business (formerly so, for Jones), and both committed to poetry (each in our own way). But these are points of synchronicity (to borrow a term from the New Agers) that occur randomly in the lives of otherwise unconnected people. Might as well stand outside the local ice cream parlor and intercept the next person coming out with two scoops of pralines and cream and pronounce you are star-crossed because that's your favorite flavor, too.

Elizabeth Biller, whose perceptive psychological assessment of Jones helped me better understand him, offered a slightly different turn to the dance-of-opposites theory. Noting Jones made specific mention in one of his communications with McKee about being treated kindly by me when he sent poems for editorial consideration at *Poet & Critic*, she remarked, "I hate to think, but do indeed conclude, that your unusual willingness to extend yourself may have made you a more likely target for this dreadful person to aim at and pursue." While this notion helps explain why Jones selected me as his special victim for sustained abuse, it makes me feel rather like a wildebeest browsing upwind of the lions.

Even if I reject these theories as fanciful and conclude Jones found me entirely by chance and might have settled on some other poor soul had he picked up another periodical on another day, the fact that we are now linked is unchanged. Had I kept quiet about him, concealing him like a family embarrassment, I could have diminished the awareness of our association, but I could not have prevented the personal damage done me by the fundamental act of plagiarism itself. Whether or not leaving him relatively free to plagiarize at will might have kept him from doing worse things is something I worry about. Of course, making him a gift of the poems would have deprived him of the pleasure he took in stealing them; and that, too, might have turned him in a worse direction. Fretting in this way about causal possibilities has no end other than arterial plaque, and I have accumulated my share of it.

Whether or not telling the story will help, I can't say. Perhaps in the end, Jones's greatest challenge to me has not been to fight for the words in my poems but to find the words that will explain why those poems matter to me. If I fail to meet this challenge, I will truly have been robbed, not just of my language but of a central part of my identity as well.